THE OPEN BOOK SERIES

SCIENCE & TECHNOLOGY

Edited by Alan Taman

Matter – Atoms and Molecules – Solids and Crystals – Liquids – Coal – Metals and Metalloids – Acids and Bases – Iron and Steel – the Chemical Industry – Chemical Energy – Science and Technology at Work

HODDER AND STOUGHTON
LONDON SYDNEY AUCKLAND TORONTO

British Library Cataloguing in Publication Data

Taman, Alan
  Science & technology. – (The Open book series)
  1. Science – Juvenile literature
  I. Taman, Alan   II. Series
  500   Q163

  ISBN 0-340-34476-8
  ISBN 0-340-34475-X (Pbk)

Copyright © 1981 Gruppo Editoriale Fabbri S.p.A.,
Milano – Le Livre de Paris S.A. – Hachette,
Bagneux

English language edition copyright © 1985
Hodder and Stoughton Ltd

First published in this edition 1985

Published by Hodder and Stoughton Children's Books,
a division of Hodder and Stoughton Ltd, Mill Road,
Dunton Green, Sevenoaks, Kent TN13 2YJ

Photoset by Rowland Phototypesetting Ltd,
Bury St Edmunds, Suffolk

Printed in Belgium by Henri Proost et Cie,
Turnhout

Science is concerned with finding out about things! Scientists search for information about the world we live in, the air that surrounds it, the rocks that make up its crust, the animals and plants that exist on it. Science is the search for knowledge. At the very basis of science is matter. Everything we can see and all the gases that are invisible to the naked eye are composed of matter. Even our bodies are composed of matter, as are the stars that we can see in the night sky. The branch of science that studies matter and the interaction of different types of it is called chemistry.

Matter

THE ATOMIC THEORY

A straightforward definition of matter is 'the substance or substances of which a physical object is made'.

Ever since man developed intelligence, the question of what 'matter' is has fascinated philosophers. As far back as the sixth century BC a Greek philosopher, Thales, stated his belief that all living things were made or derived from water.

A century later, another Greek claimed that water was only one of the four elements that he believed composed matter. The other three were earth, fire and air, and all substances were made up of these four elements in varying proportions.

A little later, yet another Greek philosopher, Democritus, gave us the correct answer. He argued that all matter is composed of small, hard particles which varied in size and shape and which were indestructible. It was of no importance if the substance was liquid, gas or solid. It was the way in which the particles were arranged that gave the matter its specific properties. We now call these particles atoms.

Scientifically backed proof of the atomic theory came many hundreds of years later when John Dalton, an English schoolmaster, carried out careful experiments that proved that all chemical elements – the basic materials from which all naturally occurring substances are made – are composed of atoms of one type.

An atom is the smallest part of an element that shows its chemical properties. Some elements are made up of single atoms, others exist as atoms joined together to form molecules of the element. Atoms of one element also join with those of another element to form molecules of a chemical compound.

CHEMICAL COMPOUNDS

Suppose that crystals of sugar were ground down as finely as possible. The smallest particle that will show the characteristics of sugar is a single molecule. But that molecule can be broken down further into separate atoms of hydrogen, carbon and oxygen – sugar is composed of these three elements.

The properties of the compound are different from its component elements. Sugar is white, or brown, and crumbly; carbon can be a black solid and hydrogen and oxygen are colourless gases.

Salt is another common household product that is a chemical compound. It is composed of sodium and chlorine. It would be cumbersome if scientists had to write the full name of each chemical element when describing an experiment, so each one has been given an abbreviated symbol. Salt is made up of one atom of sodium and one of chlorine. The chemical symbol for sodium is Na and for chlorine Cl: the chemical formula for salt is NaCl.

Left: under laboratory conditions, an industrial chemist controls a chemical experiment, watching closely to see the reaction.

This formula shows not only what the constituent elements are, but also how many atoms of each element make up one molecule of the substance – only one atom of each element is present in one molecule of salt. The chemical formula for water is H_2O which tells you that a molecule of water is made up of two atoms of hydrogen (H) and one of oxygen (O).

How elements join

An atom contains electrons, each of which has a negative charge. Some of these are easily removed and the remainder of the atom (the ion) is more stable without it. The atoms of other elements welcome the unwanted electron and the two are joined together in ionic (or electrovalent) bonding.

For example, when sodium combines with chlorine to form salt, the sodium sheds its unwanted negative charge which is welcomed by the chlorine. The sodium has become positively charged and the chlorine has acquired a negative charge. The two atoms are held together by the attraction that exists between unlike charges.

Another type of bonding occurs when two atoms share a pair of electrons. Each atom donates one electron to the bond rather than one giving and the other receiving. Such bonding is known as covalent bonding.

The ability of atoms to make these chemical bonds with other atoms is called valency, and the electrons that are able to form them are valency electrons.

Above: a nebula in the constellation Serpens contains more than 90% hydrogen, the most abundant element in the universe.

Below: when dilute hydrochloric acid is added to iron pyrites, the iron in the iron pyrites reacts with the chlorine in the acid to form iron chloride and the hydrogen in the acid reacts with the sulphur in the pyrites giving off the foul-smelling gas, hydrogen sulphide. When the tap is opened, the gas escapes into the beaker which contains a solution of cadmium sulphate and reacts with it to give cadmium sulphide, which is used as a yellow pigment. These small-scale reactions are repeated on a large scale in the chemical industry.

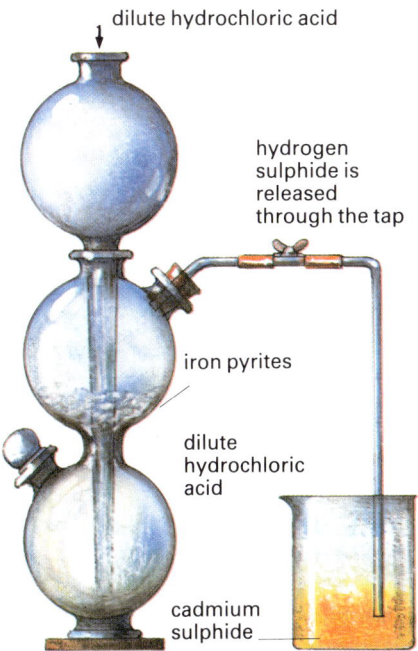

dilute hydrochloric acid

hydrogen sulphide is released through the tap

iron pyrites

dilute hydrochloric acid

cadmium sulphide

CHEMICAL REACTIONS

When two substances combine to form a new chemical, this is called a chemical reaction.

When a compound is split into its component elements by heat, this is called a decomposition reaction.

Other reactions are the double decomposition reaction (for example, when silver nitrate reacts with potassium chloride two new substances are created – silver chloride and potassium nitrate); and the replacement reaction, which occurs when an atom takes the place of another atom in a compound.

You can see a replacement reaction for yourself if you dip an iron bar into a solution of copper sulphate ($CuSO_4$). The iron (Fe) takes the place of the copper in the copper sulphate and the displaced copper (Cu) is deposited on the iron as rust. The solution becomes iron sulphate ($FeSO_4$). A chemist describes this with a chemical equation:

$$Fe + CuSO_4 \rightarrow FeSO_4 + Cu$$

Left: a petrochemical complex, where crude oil is broken down and subjected to the various processes necessary to change it into a vast range of products.

4

NATURALLY OCCURRING ELEMENTS

Element	Symbol	Atomic number	Element	Symbol	Atomic number	Element	Symbol	Atomic number
Actinium	Ac	89	Hydrogen	H	1	Radium	Ra	88
Aluminium	Al	13	Indium	In	49	Radon	Rn	86
Antimony	Sb	51	Iodine	I	53	Rhenium	Re	75
Argon	Ar	18	Iridium	Ir	77	Rhodium	Rh	45
Arsenic	As	33	Iron	Fe	26	Rubidium	Rb	37
Astatine	At	85	Krypton	Kr	36	Ruthenium	Ru	44
Barium	Ba	56	Lanthanum	La	57	Samarium	Sm	62
Beryllium	Be	4	Lead	Pb	82	Scandium	Sc	21
Bismuth	Bi	83	Lithium	Li	3	Selenium	Se	34
Boron	B	5	Lutetium	Lu	71	Silicon	Si	14
Bromine	Br	35	Magnesium	Mg	12	Silver	Ag	47
Cadmium	Cd	48	Manganese	Mn	25	Sodium	Na	11
Caesium	Cs	55	Mercury	Hg	80	Strontium	Sr	38
Calcium	Ca	20	Molybdenum	Mo	42	Sulphur	S	16
Carbon	C	6	Neodymium	Nd	60	Tantalum	Ta	73
Cerium	Ce	58	Neon	Ne	10	Technetium	Tc	43
Chlorine	Cl	17	Neptunium	Np	93	Tellurium	Te	52
Chromium	Cr	24	Nickel	Ni	28	Terbium	Tb	65
Cobalt	Co	27	Niobium	Nb	41	Thallium	Tl	81
Copper	Cu	29	Nitrogen	N	7	Thorium	Th	90
Dysprosium	Dy	66	Osmium	Os	76	Thulium	Tm	69
Erbium	Er	68	Oxygen	O	8	Tin	Sn	50
Europium	Eu	63	Palladium	Pd	46	Titanium	Ti	22
Fluorine	F	9	Phosphorus	P	15	Tungsten	W	74
Francium	Fr	87	Platinum	Pt	78	Uranium	U	92
Gadolinium	Gd	64	Plutonium	Pu	94	Vanadium	V	23
Gallium	Ga	31	Polonium	Po	84	Xenon	Xe	54
Germanium	Ge	32	Potassium	K	19	Ytterbium	Yb	70
Gold	Au	79	Praseodymium	Pr	59	Yttrium	Y	39
Hafnium	Hf	72	Promethium	Pm	61	Zinc	Zn	30
Helium	He	2	Protactinium	Pa	91	Zirconium	Zr	40
Holmium	Ho	67						

Below: the Periodic Table. The elements all have their own symbols and are arranged in vertical groups and horizontal periods in order of their atomic numbers. Elements that have similar properties are grouped together in vertical columns, and going across the table from left to right the elements become less metallic in nature, eventually becoming non-metals.

Group O, at the end, is composed of the rare, or noble, gases. From its position in the table, an element's properties can easily be predicted.

The Lanthanides are a group of rare metallic elements which resemble aluminium, and the Actinides form a group of radioactive elements – most of which are man-made – known as the transuranium elements.

Above: when wood burns, the elements of which it is chiefly composed – carbon, oxygen and hydrogen – react with the elements in the air to form carbon dioxide and water. This is an example of oxidation.

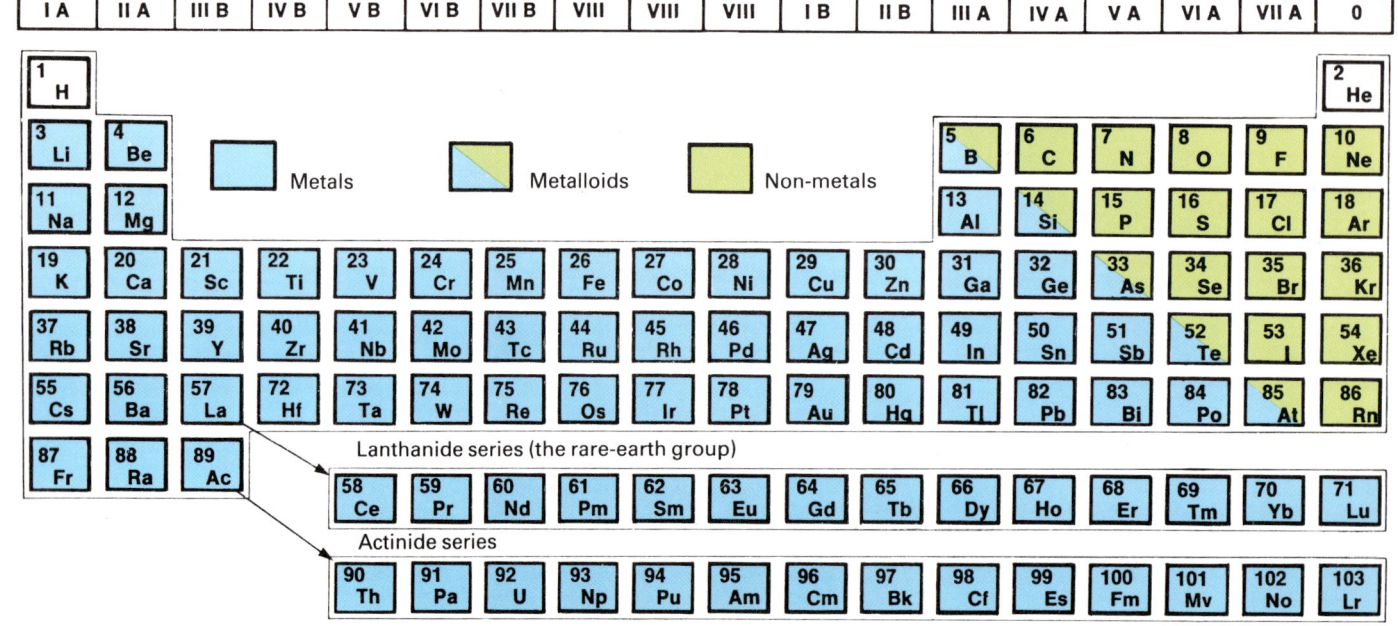

THE ELEMENTS

The founder of modern chemistry was an Irish aristocrat, Robert Boyle (1627–91). Before he began his experiments, scientists had had a vague idea that some metals could be made into others and there were also theories that matter could be resolved into simple units. Boyle was the first to prove that an element was something that could not be changed into anything simpler.

The number of elements of which Boyle was aware was comparatively small. We now know that there are 94 naturally occurring elements.

As more became known, it gradually became obvious that some of the elements had similar characteristics, and some of the interested scientists began to wonder if they could be tabulated so that those with similar properties could be grouped together.

Despite their size, each atom is made up of even smaller particles. It has a central nucleus composed of neutrons and protons and an outer part containing a number of electrons which equals the number of protons in the nucleus. This number is the element's atomic number. Hydrogen, for example, has one electron and one proton, and was thus given the atomic number 1. Scientists were also able to assign an atomic weight to each element, which takes into account the number of neutrons in the atom. The atomic weight of hydrogen is 1.008.

The Periodic Table

In 1869 D. I. Mendeleev, a Russian physicist, proposed the Periodic Table of Elements, organised in order of their ascending atomic weight. There had been attempts so to organise the elements before, but Mendeleev's table was different – it had gaps in it. Where there was a large disparity in the weights of two neighbouring elements, Mendeleev assumed that there was a yet-to-be discovered element between the two. He was proved to be correct when the elements he predicted were finally identified.

The modern Periodic Table arranges the elements in order of their atomic numbers, in vertical groups and horizontal periods.

MAN-MADE ELEMENTS

By bombarding an element with neutrons, scientists can create elements, known as transuranium elements.

Fourteen have been created in the last fifty years, two of which, neptunium (93) and plutonium (94) have since been found, in minute traces, as naturally occurring elements. The three most recent discoveries, not shown on the Periodic Table opposite, are unnilquadium (also called rutherfordium or kurchatovium), unnilpentium (also called hahnium or nielsborium) and unnilhexium. One American scientist has predicted over 100 transuranium elements.

The twelve known man-made elements are:

Element	Symbol	Atomic number
Americium	Am	95
Berkelium	Bk	97
Californium	Cf	98
Curium	Cm	96
Einsteinium	Es	99
Fermium	Fm	100
Lawrencium	Lr	103
Mendelevium	Md	101
Nobelium	No	102
Unnilhexium	Unh	106
Unnilpentium	Unp	105
Unnilquadium	Unq	104

SYNTHETIC MATERIALS

Far from being content with the number of elements and compounds that occur naturally, scientists have created many new materials, many of which play a vital part in our lives. The most important are the plastics which are found in many part of our houses, in our clothes – almost everywhere.

The molecules of plastics contain long chains of carbon atoms – polymers – that give the plastics their peculiar properties. Polymers are either thermosetting or thermoplastic. In the former, the long chains of atoms are linked, with the result that they cannot slide over each other. These are the hard, heat-resistant plastics. The chains of atoms in thermoplastic polymers can slide over each other when heated, making the plastics easy to mould and re-shape.

Many of our plastics and other chemicals come from petroleum, a mixture of many different chemicals. These are separated at an oil refinery and used to give us plastics, drugs, explosives, dyes and fertilisers, as well as petrol.

LIQUIDS AND GASES

Some substances are solid, others are liquid, and yet others are gaseous. Why is this? As we have seen, all matter is composed of atoms which are held together to form molecules. In a solid, all of the molecules occupy a fixed position (they can oscillate – but their position relative to each other is stable) and the substances retain the same shape unless an external force is brought to bear on them (see page 13). In liquids, however, the molecules are free to move about, giving the liquids the ability to change shape. The molecules remain close to each other but can slide past each other. This allows the liquid to adopt the shape of its container. Molecules of gases move away from each other whenever they can. Gases therefore tend to expand indefinitely. Changes in temperature have a marked effect on gases. Experiments have shown that, if pressure remains constant, the volume of a gas increases by $1/273$ of its volume at 0 °C for each 1 °C rise in temperature. Reduction in temperature – at constant pressure – results in a loss of volume.

Above: carbon is one of the most important and versatile of elements. It occurs naturally as diamond, as seen here, as graphite and as amorphous carbon (gas-carbon, lamp-black, etc.). The phenomenon of occurring in different forms is known as allotropy.

POLLUTION

The importance of the chemical industry in the twentieth century cannot be overestimated. We depend on chemistry and the careful control of chemical reactions to provide many of the products that we consider essential – petrol, plastics and a whole range of petrochemical materials. Unfortunately, the growth in the chemical industry has resulted in widespread pollution in many parts of the world.

Toxic substances belch out of industrial chimneys into the atmosphere, often reacting with the gases present there to form deadly poisons that fall back to Earth as acid rain. The widespread damage that this causes, especially to historic buildings and monuments, has become a major concern, so much so that international conferences, attended by leading politicians from many countries, are now held to discuss the most efficient ways of controlling it.

Chemical waste products are also pumped into rivers, rendering them sterile and upsetting the ecological balance. Europe's major waterway, the Rhine, is now heavily polluted for much of its course.

Fortunately, conservationists have managed to bring the dangers of over-pollution to the world's attention and steps have been taken to prevent it. The river Timiş, flowing through Romania, was for a long time completely polluted, but now, thanks to strict controls and expensive treatment, life has been restored to the water and the river is once again the home of trout and other fish that had long ago been killed by the pollution.

THE LARGEST LABORATORY

What do you think of if you try to picture a chemical laboratory? A large industrial plant as illustrated on page 3, or the science lab at school with its gas taps, bunsen burners, retort stands and other equipment?

Many scientists say that the universe itself is a huge chemical laboratory in which millions upon millions of chemical reactions are constantly taking place – some simple, others extremely complex.

Here are some examples:

The formation of rust on submerged hulls of ships, caused by the reaction of the metal with the salts and minerals in the seawater.
The way in which the inside of a potato turns brown when it is exposed to air.
The decomposition of cut grass and other vegetation into compost.
The way in which white paper turns yellow if it is left in the sunlight.

Life – animal, vegetable and mineral – is a non-stop series of chemical reactions.

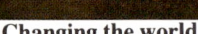

Below: iron rusts if it is overexposed to moist air. This is caused by a reaction of the hydrogen and oxygen in the moist air with the iron, which produces a hydrated oxide of the iron. This is more than a mere inconvenience to motorists, it is also an expense. If rust could be efficiently and economically controlled the saving would be enormous; more than 20% of all iron produced is used to replace that which is lost as rust.

Changing the world

Because many of the natural chemical reactions that occur in the world take place over a very long time, we are unaware of them, but as time passes many of them are changing the face of the Earth. The familiar stalactites and stalagmites are a good example of this. If we were to enter a cave over two successive days we would not notice any difference, but if we were able to go into a cave one day and return to it 10,000 years later we would be immediately aware of the difference. Solid, icicle-like formations would be reaching down from the roof and upwards from the ground. The forces of chemistry have been slowly, but visibly, at work.

The combination of the physical action of waves and the chemical reaction of the salts in the water and the minerals in the rocks, changes the very appearance of the coastline. The ancient Britons who lived in what is now Dorset would hardly recognise the cliffs and coves of the present-day shore.

The chemical reaction that occurs when minerals in the earth cause natural debris to fossilise can provide geologists with valuable clues as to what life on Earth was like long before man appeared on the scene.

Essential for man's survival

Every living organism depends on chemical reactions. When these cease life dies.

Our bodies are the scene of countless chemical reactions, extracting essential nutrients from the food we eat, converting them into substances that the body needs for its growth and existence. The chemical processes occurring within living organisms are referred to as metabolism, and can be classified as those that break down complex substances with the release of energy, essential for the organisms' activities (catabolism), and those that build up complex substances with the absorption or storage of energy (anabolism).

The chemical reactions occurring in plants are essential to us, for we would cease to exist without photosynthesis as all the food that we eat has its origins in the process. Photosynthesis enables the plant to manufacture its own foodstuffs from water and carbon dioxide (the gas that we exhale) using the energy derived from sunlight. The by-product of the process is oxygen (which the plant expires) – the very gas that we depend on. This is one of the reasons why conservationists are so concerned about the rate at which some parts of the world are being deforested. It is estimated that every minute of every day, fourteen acres (5.6 hectares) of tropical rain forest are destroyed. Not only does this threaten the animals that live there, it also reduces the plant kingdom's capacity to produce life-supporting oxygen.

Chemistry is not just a tedious academic subject – it is the very basis of life.

Above: the caves of Castellani in Bari, southern Italy. The magnificent stalagmites and stalactites are formed by the presence of calcium carbonate in droplets of water that form in the caves. If the droplets hang in the same place before falling, a film of carbonate is deposited as the water evaporates. Successive layers of this film grow into stalactites. If the water drops on the same spot on the floor, upward-growing stalagmites are formed. Sometimes they join up to form pillars of calcium carbonate.

The rate of growth varies. Some of these formations may have taken 2,000 years or more to reach their present length. But in the Ingleborough Cave in Yorkshire it took only ten years for one stalactite to grow by 7·6 centimetres (3 inches).

Right: a handkerchief tree, Davidia involucrata, *in the sunshine. The presence of sunlight on green plants enables them to perform the highly complex chemical reaction that allows the plants to manufacture their own food – carbohydrates – from carbon dioxide and water.*

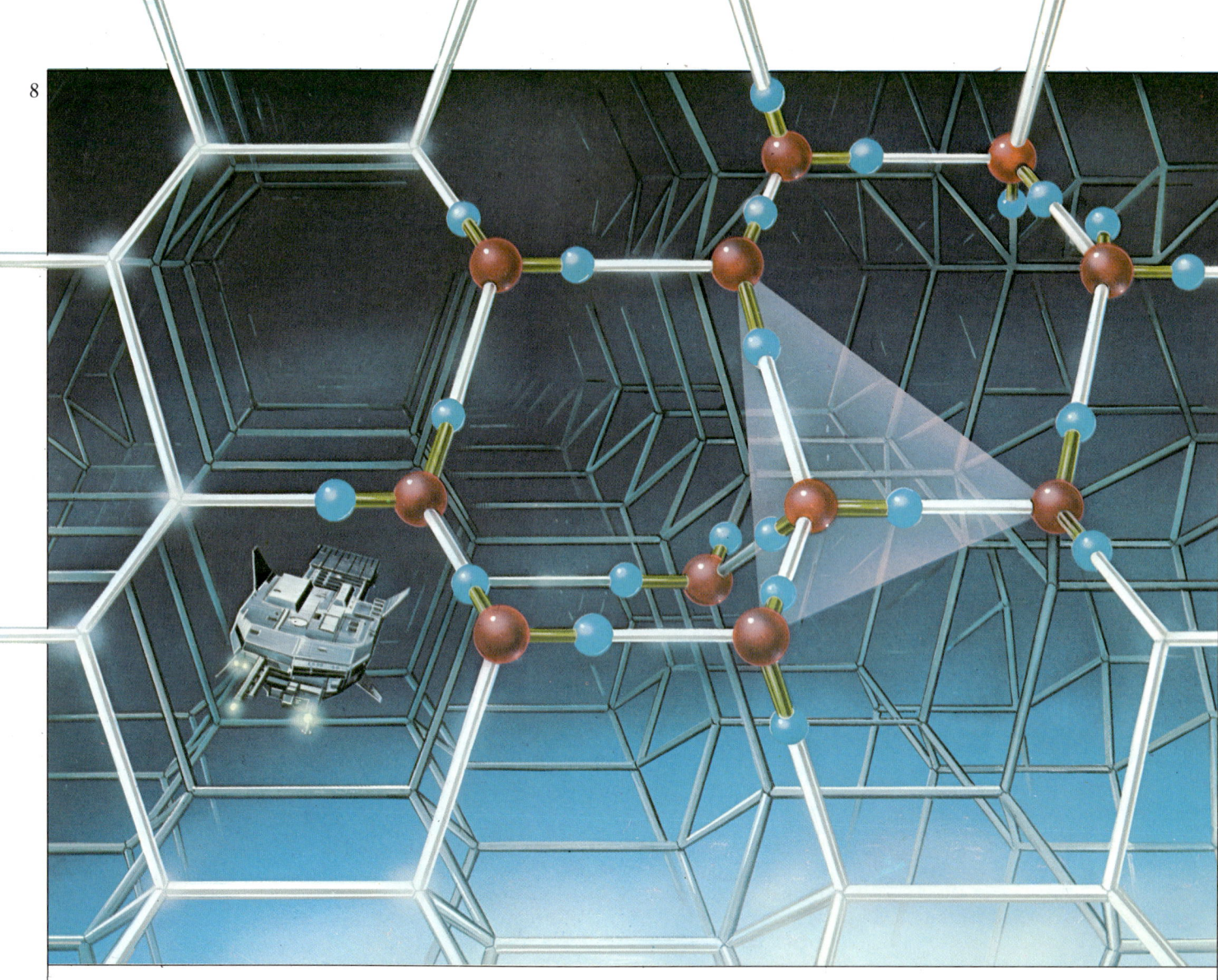

Atoms and Molecules

This spacecraft travelling through a weird landscape is not an artist's impression of a journey to a strange planet, but a representation of what an astronaut in a miniaturised spaceship would see if his journey took him into ice and he could see the molecular structure of the water. Atoms of oxygen are linked to atoms of hydrogen to form molecules of water. One oxygen atom (red) and two of hydrogen (blue) are held together by electrostatic attraction (here represented by the yellow links). The individual molecules are linked together (represented by the white lines). It would take many millions of such linked molecules to form a droplet of water that we could see. The pink triangle shows the area of force that holds the molecules together.

THE STRUCTURE OF THE ATOM

Atom comes to us from a Greek word which means indivisible – an appropriate link when we remember that for many centuries scientists considered that atoms were the smallest particles of matter.

We now know differently. An atom is not an indivisible solid but a hollow shell containing a fixed nucleus (which is itself made up of smaller parts) around which are a varying number of moving particles, the electrons.

Our knowledge of atomic structure took a great leap forwards when, in 1897, a British physicist, J. J. Thomson, announced the results of his experiments. Thomson established the existence of minute negatively charged electrical particles, which he called 'corpuscles'. These were light in weight even when compared to hydrogen atoms, the lightest known particles at the time. These corpuscles were later named electrons.

In 1902, another British physicist by the name of Thomson, William Thomson (later

Lord Kelvin), pictured the atom as a positively charged sphere with electrons attached to its surface (figure 1, opposite). In 1904 J. J. Thomson stated that the electrons were inside the sphere, and showed how they would arrange themselves.

A Japanese scientist, Nagaoka, put forward a theory that compared the structure of the atom to a planetary system, a theory which became the basis for all future models. Nagaoka thought that the atom was formed of a central, positively charged particle, around which the electrons moved in a single circular orbit (figure 2).

This theory was taken a stage further by Ernest Rutherford, a New Zealand physicist who was one of J. J. Thomson's students, and who succeeded to the Chair of Natural Philosophy at Cambridge when Thomson retired. Rutherford supposed that atoms were composed of a small central nucleus with a positive charge, which accounted for most of the atom's weight, around which were scattered the negatively charged electrons in a sphere of a radius comparable with the size of the atom, the number of electrons being exactly sufficient to balance the positive charge of the nucleus (figure 3). He then demonstrated the existence of the nucleus.

In Rutherford's theory, most of the volume of the atom is empty space, while Thomson's model assumed that the positive charge filled the volume of the atom.

Rutherford came to his conclusion after directing a stream of alpha rays at a piece of thin gold foil. As most of them passed straight through, he deduced that the gold atoms were mostly empty space which presented no barrier to the rays.

Niels Bohr, a Danish physicist, agreed with Rutherford, but he thought that the electrons moved around the nucleus, not in a circular chain as described by Nagaoka, but in their own individual circular paths, rather like a miniature solar system. During 1915 and 1916 A. Sommerfeld, a German, refined Bohr's theory, declaring that the electron paths were elliptical rather than circular (figure 4).

We know that the Bohr/Sommerfeld model is too simple. Electrons do not travel in the regular fashion described by these two scientists, and rather than following well-defined orbits they fly out in all directions, although they do tend to remain at a predictable distance from the nucleus. The result is a nucleus surrounded by clouds of electrical charge formed by the electrons travelling at immense speeds.

Returning to the comparison between atomic structure and the orbit of the planets around the Sun, we now know that this is not valid. Rather than the planetary orbits of a solar system, the effect created by the movement of electrons around the nucleus is that of a stellar nebula (figure 5).

electrons

1

Thomson's atom

2

Nagaoka's atom

nucleus

orbital path

3

Rutherford's atom

4

Bohr/Sommerfeld atom

electron cloud

5

Atom as seen by modern scientists

MEASURING THE ATOM

Despite their small size, atoms have definable dimensions which vary from element to element. The radius ranges from 0·5 to 3 hundred millionths of a centimetre. The international unit of measurement used is the Ångström (Å), which is one ten millionth of a millimetre (10^{-10} m).

The nucleus is itself composed of smaller units – protons and neutrons. The strength of the nucleus's positive charge is decided by the number of protons, which also determines the element's atomic number. The number of protons is the same in every atom of an element, but the number of neutrons can vary. Atoms of elements where there is such a difference create isotopes of the element. Isotopes of the same element have identical chemical properties, but differ slightly in their physical properties. The majority of isotopes are unstable and radioactive; they are usually called radioisotopes. Carbon-14 is a naturally occurring radioisotope, as are uranium-233, 235 and 238.

A HUGE DROP OF WATER

If it were possible to have a drop of water the same size as the Earth, one of the component molecules among the hundreds of millions of which the drop would be made up would be approximately the same size as a hazelnut. But the atoms of which they are composed would still be invisible to the naked eye.

Below are the dimensions of some simple molecular substances composed of one, two or three atoms. The number alongside the substance indicates the angstrom value.

Hydrogen	0·7
Lithium	2·6
Sodium	3·0
Potassium	3·9
Hydrochloric acid	1·2
Hydrobromic acid	1·4
Hydriodic acid	1·6
Calcium fluoride	2·3
Oxygen	1·2
Carbon monoxide	1·1
Water	2·5
Nitric oxide	1·1
Sodium hydroxide	1·8
Iodine	2·6
Hydrogen sulphide	2·0
Calcium sulphate	2·0
Deuterium	0·7
Chlorine	1·9
Bromine	2·2

The variations, as you can see, are huge, ranging from 0·7 to 3·9 – potassium atoms are more than five times larger than hydrogen atoms. Returning to our huge imaginary drop of water: if the molecules of water are the size of a hazelnut, then a molecule of potassium on the same scale would be the size of an apricot.

It is quite extraordinary that scientists have been able to establish as much information as they have about atomic structure, considering the size of a single atom.

Atomic physics have been beneficial to man. By harnessing the power of the atom, scientists have given us a new and important source of energy which is more widely used as fossil fuel reserves are being exhausted.

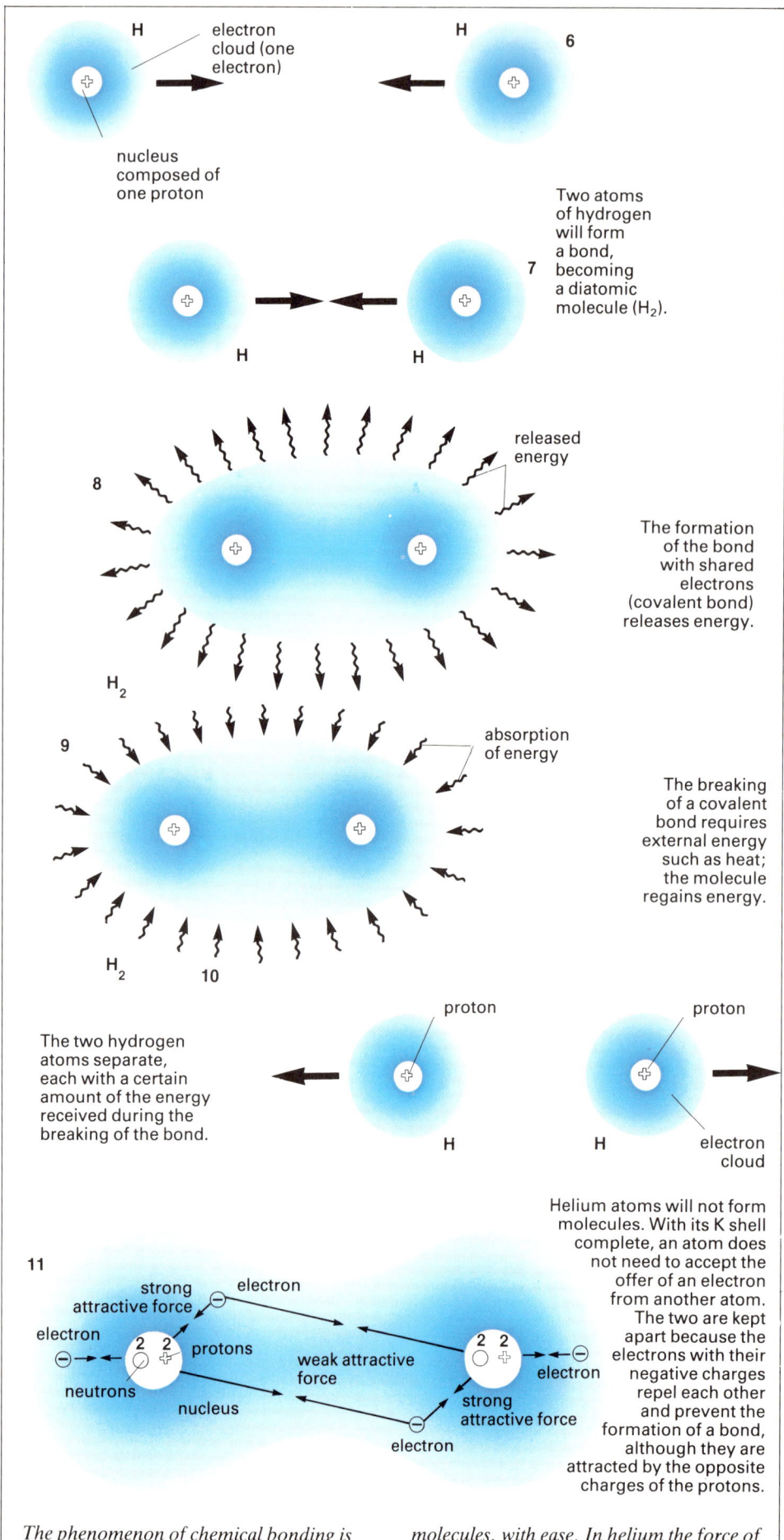

10

6 — H, electron cloud (one electron), nucleus composed of one proton, H

Two atoms of hydrogen will form a bond, becoming a diatomic molecule (H$_2$). **7**

8 released energy. The formation of the bond with shared electrons (covalent bond) releases energy. H$_2$

9 absorption of energy. The breaking of a covalent bond requires external energy such as heat; the molecule regains energy. H$_2$ **10**

The two hydrogen atoms separate, each with a certain amount of the energy received during the breaking of the bond.

proton — H, electron cloud, proton — H

Helium atoms will not form molecules. With its K shell complete, an atom does not need to accept the offer of an electron from another atom. The two are kept apart because the electrons with their negative charges repel each other and prevent the formation of a bond, although they are attracted by the opposite charges of the protons.

11 strong attractive force, electron, electron, 2 2 protons, neutrons, nucleus, weak attractive force, 2 2 electron, strong attractive force, electron

MOLECULES

Molecules are formed when atoms come together and combine to create molecules of the element of which they are atoms, for example hydrogen, or to create new compounds, in which case the molecule is the smallest particle to retain the unique properties of the compound.

As we have seen, the electrons move around the nucleus. In doing so they form a 'shell'. The inner shell never holds more than two electrons. When the first shell is full, a second shell is formed which can hold eight electrons, and if there are more than that number a third shell is formed, and so on. Shells are designated the letters K to Q outwards from the nucleus. It is the outermost shell that holds the valency, or bonding, electrons and is therefore important in the creation of molecules.

Hydrogen is unique. It is the only atom that has no neutrons in its nucleus and does not have two electrons in its K shell: the shell is only partially filled, making it chemically unstable. The hydrogen could throw off its single electron and become a proton, but more commonly forms a diatomic molecule with another hydrogen atom. This is known as H$_2$. The two electrons are now shared by both atoms. The K shell is complete (figures 6 and 7).

The two electrons move rapidly around the atoms, spending so much time between the nuclei that the atoms are held together by the electrical attraction that is present. The formation of H$_2$ is an example of covalent bonding – two atoms sharing a pair of electrons, one being donated by each atom. This bond is illustrated in figures 8 and 9.

The bond is so strong that if it is to be broken, strong external energy such as heat is required before the H$_2$ molecule separates and the two atoms move away from each other (figure 10).

The next element in the Periodic Table, helium, is chemically stable. Its K shell has its full complement of two electrons. Two atoms of helium that come together will not form a covalent bond as does hydrogen. Electrons, with their negative charges, repel each other unless there is a space in the shell to fill (figure 11). Helium is one of the rare, or noble, gases which were once thought unique in the chemical world because of their apparent unwillingness to combine with other elements to form compounds. In 1962, however, a breakthrough was achieved and since then many fluorides, oxides and other compounds of xenon, krypton and radon have been made. So far, however, compounds of helium have not been made. At a temperature of 2K helium undergoes a transition from liquid helium 1 to liquid helium 2. This spreads in layers a few atoms thick, which has been described by some scientists as flowing uphill, as it will actually run up the sides of a container and over the top.

The phenomenon of chemical bonding is the very base of all chemistry, but not all elements form bonds, and therefore molecules, with ease. In helium the force of the electrons prevents the formation of a bond, while in hydrogen it creates one.

MORE COMPLEX MATTERS

The principle of an atom accepting electrons to complete its external shell is the same in the bonding of different elements.

Let us look at the formation of a molecule of water, H_2O, made up of two atoms of hydrogen and one of oxygen. The diatomic hydrogen molecule has two electrons and the oxygen atom has eight, two of which are in the K shell. The other six are in the next shell, arranged as two complementary pairs and two individual atoms. When hydrogen and oxygen come together, the two 'single' electrons in the oxygen atom's second shell 'marry' the two electrons in the H_2 molecule, giving the shell of the oxygen atom its full complement of eight electrons – two of which it shares with the H_2 molecule (figures 12 and 13). The chemical formula, $H_2 + O \rightarrow H_2O$, shows that the diatomic hydrogen molecule, H_2, has combined with the single atom of oxygen, O, forming H_2O. Figure 13 also shows how the two hydrogen electrons have been rejected by the paired oxygen electrons but accepted by the two single ones, creating an angle of 105 degrees between the atoms.

Figures 14 and 15 show a molecule of methane, the simplest alkane (the general name of hydrocarbons of the methane series). Methane, or colourless, odourless gas, is formed when one atom of carbon bonds with four hydrogen atoms. Figure 15 shows that the resulting structure is tetrahedral, with angles of 109·5 degrees.

In figure 16 we see a molecule of myoglobin, which is found in our bodies and is essential to our survival. The haem is an organic pigment containing ferrous iron, without which we would die.

Iron is central to the amazingly complex cytochrome molecule (figure 17) which also contains nitrogen and other elements. Cytochrome plays an essential role in the body's metabolism.

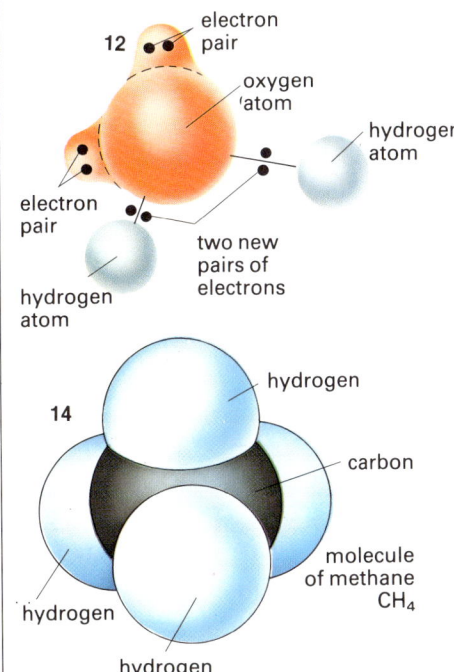

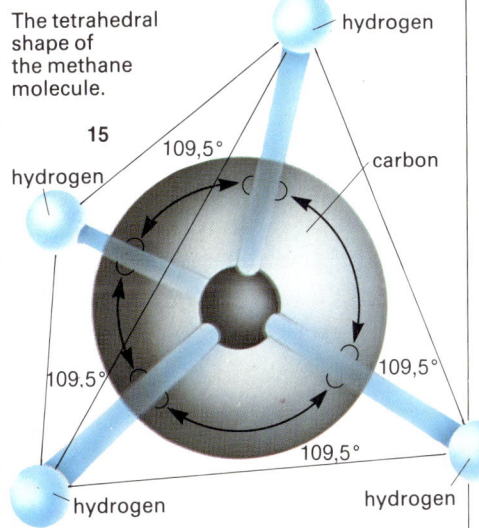

The tetrahedral shape of the methane molecule.

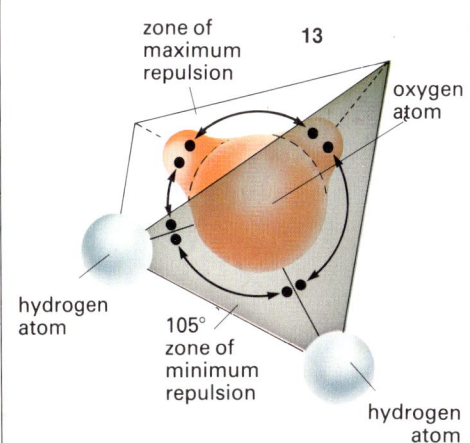

The structural organisation of chains determines the spatial characteristics of a molecule and its capacity to react with other substances.

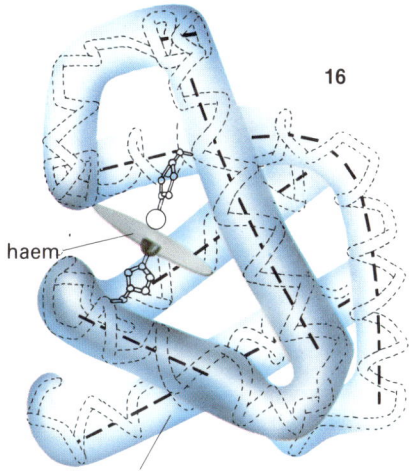

Myoglobin molecule showing the different chains of amino acids of which it is composed.

section of a cytochrome molecule

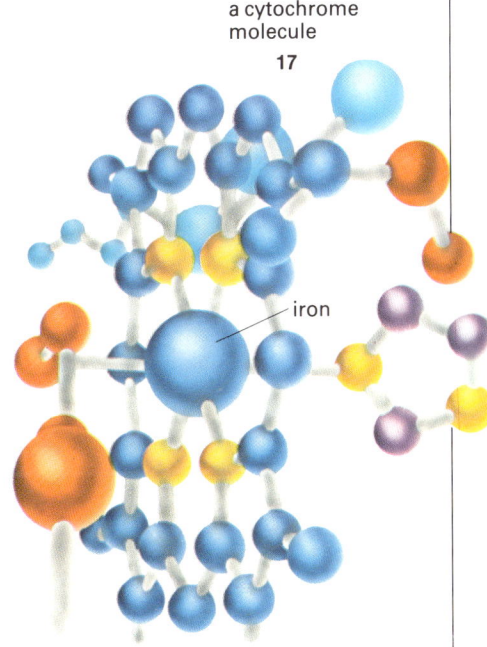

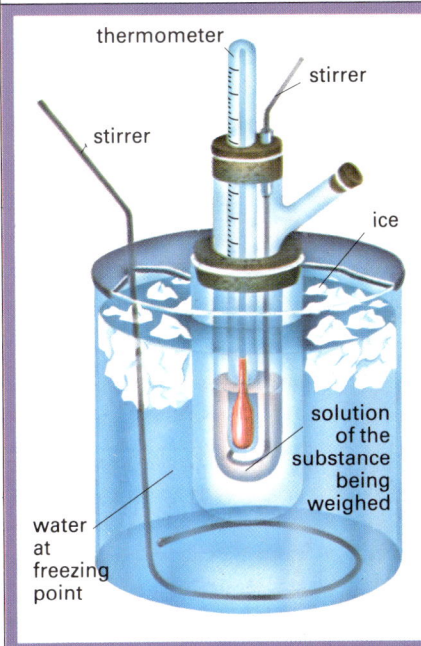

DETERMINING MOLECULAR WEIGHT

The weight of the molecules of a substance can be calculated by using a cryoscope. A weighed amount of pure solvent is placed in a tube fitted with a very sensitive thermometer, and fitted into another tube suspended in a mixture of ice and water. The solvent is cooled to freezing point and the temperature at which it freezes is noted. The tube is removed and the solvent allowed to liquefy. A weighed amount of the substance is added to the solvent through the side tube and the mixture stirred. The tube is replaced in the freezing mixture and the point at which the solution freezes is noted.

The difference between the freezing point of the pure solvent and the freezing point of the solution is used in a complicated equation which determines the weight of the molecules of the substance.

Solids and Crystals

One of Ireland's greatest tourist attractions consists of thousands of columns of basalt rock, set closely together like a giant honeycomb, forming an enormous staircase leading down to the sea. Geologists say that the Giant's Causeway was formed by the rapid cooling and cracking of an enormous lava-sheet which poured over the land several million years ago. The world of solids is one of great beauty and enormous fascination.

OPPOSING FORCES

The earth is a solid place. Its crust, both on dry land and on the ocean floor, is made up of rocks, which, like all other matter, are made up of atoms coming together to form molecules. These atoms are constantly on the move, but in solids are held together by the interaction between the molecules. They can move about in space, or oscillate, but they are unable to change their position relative to each other.

Two opposing forces are at work between molecules in equilibrium – attraction and repulsion. Simultaneously, these forces hold the molecules together and force them apart.

When a copper ring is heated, it expands because the copper molecules become excited and oscillate with more energy. As they are pushed closer to, and repelled more violently from their neighbours, the space between them increases. When enough energy is applied to a solid, the forces of attraction and repulsion that hold the molecules together are overcome and the molecules are free to move about; it loses its solid state and begins to melt – it becomes a liquid.

The solid state of matter can therefore be defined as one in which the particles occupy fixed positions, giving the substance definite shape, which it retains until it is subject to external forces.

There are two types of solids – those that are crystalline with a definite melting point, and those that are amorphous with no definite melting point.

THE ORIGINS OF ROCK

A walk along the seashore well illustrates the infinite variety of rock that is present in the world. A grain of sand and the towering cliffs that dominate the coastline are both rock. The forces of nature and the chemical make-up of the rock combine to mould each fragment into a unique specimen.

Rock is formed by one of three processes. Igneous rock begins as magma. Thousands of millions of years ago, the surface of the Earth was so hot that there was only molten material. Today, magma originates deep within the Earth, often ascending to the surface during volcanic activity.

Sedimentary rock is formed by the relentless process of weathering, where the Earth's crust is gradually eroded by wind and rain and by the chemicals present in the soil and atmosphere. As it is worn down, the particles produced accumulate in low-lying areas or on the bed of a lake or the sea. Here they combine with organic detritus (worn-down matter) such as cast-off shells. When they are compacted and hardened, these sediments are converted to sandstone, shale and limestone.

Rocks change their mineral content and texture according to their environment; metamorphic rock is the result of changes in the molecular structure of igneous or sedimentary rock. This phenomenon is most common where the Earth's crust has folded so that great pressure is placed on the rock at higher temperatures, which produces such rocks as slate and marble.

Normally this process is a very gradual one, but there are dramatic examples of metamorphosis taking place instantaneously. The impact of a meteorite hurtling through the atmosphere and striking the Earth's surface creates a yawning crater. The extreme temperature and pressure caused by such an impact generate immediate changes in the internal structure of the surrounding rock.

Bottom: quartz is a good example of the beauty of many crystalline structures.

LOOKING AT CRYSTALS

The structure of those solids that are crystalline is not always immediately obvious. Sometimes the surface has to be polished before the crystal becomes visible, and sometimes the crystalline properties are so minute that they cannot be seen with the naked eye. However, since all minerals possess a unique chemical make-up which never varies, all crystals deriving from it will have the same shape. This is because the atoms in these solids are arranged in a regular pattern called a crystalline lattice.

Lattices form very strong networks because the molecules are bonded together like the steel girders of a sky-scraper.

The result of this bonding is a three-dimensional figure, a crystal. Looking at a piece of quartz we see many aspects or faces. To crystallographers, however, the most interesting thing about crystals is the angle between their faces. The classification of crystals is based on the mathematical relationship between these angles. The crystal systems – as the classes are called – depend on the symmetry of the angles, rather than the size or shape of the faces.

Bonding

The strength of all crystalline solids – from the diamond to the snowflake – comes from the way in which the atoms are bonded to each other within the lattice by the forces of attraction and repulsion. Bonding, as we have seen, may be ionic (electrovalent) or covalent. Crystals of sodium chloride, or salt (NaCl), are held together by the attraction of opposite charges; an example of ionic bonding. The sodium atom becomes a positively charged sodium ion (Na^+), giving up an electron to the chlorine atom which becomes a negatively charged chlorine ion (Cl^-) when it takes up the electron.

Atoms sharing electrons in the outer shell, as in those of hydrogen chloride (HCl), are held together by covalent bonding.

The smallest arrangement of atoms which makes up the basic structure of a crystal is called the unit cell. This unit cell is repeated, in exactly the same configuration, to form the crystal lattice.

The study of crystals, crystallography, began many centuries ago with the work of the Danish physicist, Niels Stenson, who studied the angles between the faces of quartz crystals. Much of our knowledge today stems from his work and, although there have been several practical applications for industry, the science remains in the realm of theoretical physics.

Right: many crystals are breathtakingly beautiful, such as those of casein (top), the main protein of milk, which is solidified by the addition of an acid. Below are the lattices of sodium chloride (salt) and pyrite (an iron ore) together with their crystals.

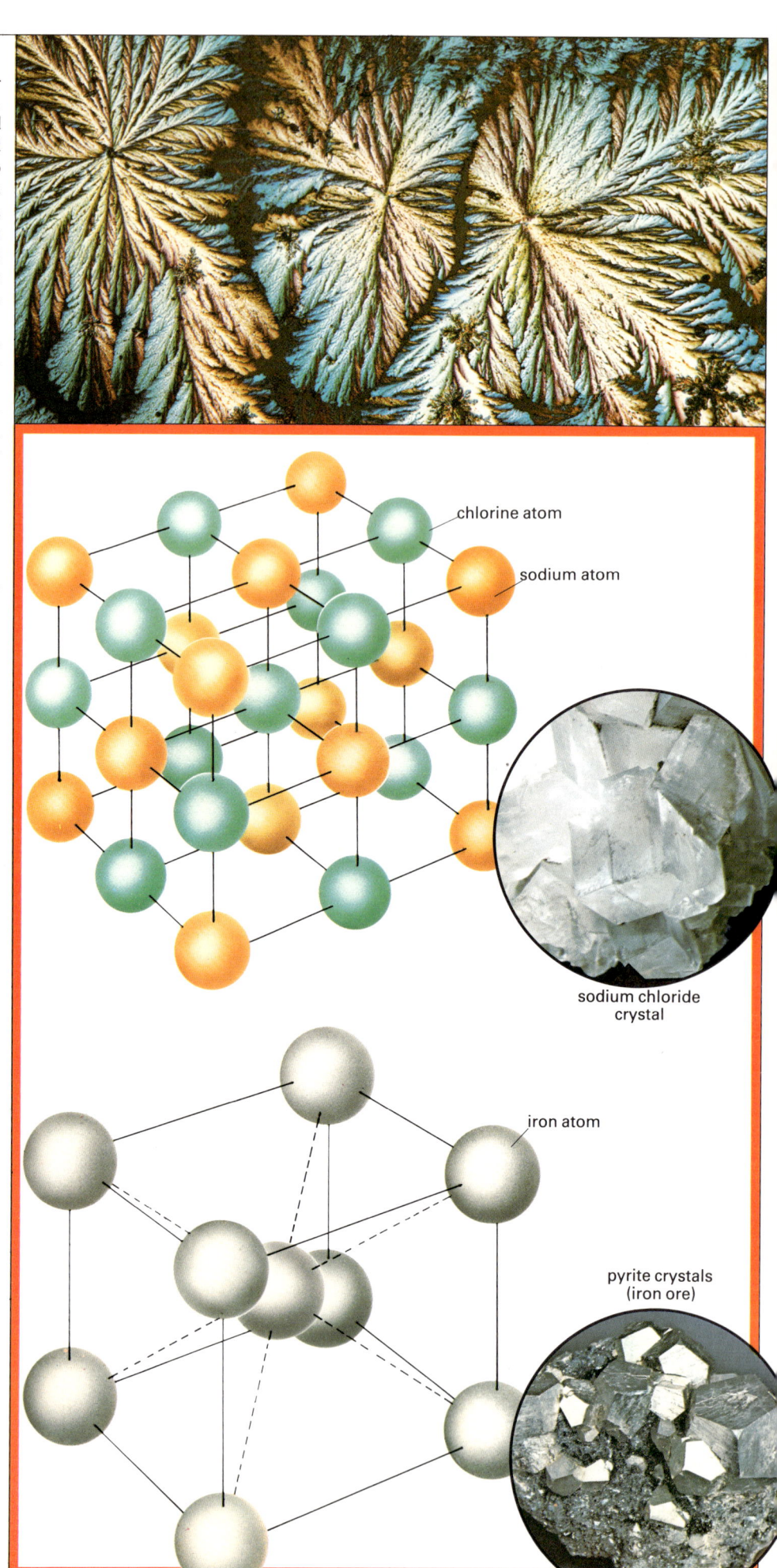

chlorine atom

sodium atom

sodium chloride crystal

iron atom

pyrite crystals (iron ore)

CARBON: ONE ELEMENT, MANY FORMS

Carbon is one of the most abundant minerals that occur in the earth and also one of the most intriguing. It combines with other substances to form more compounds than all the other elements put together. It is one of the few non-metallic substances to be found in its pure state – that is, in a natural state.

In its pure, crystalline state, carbon occurs both as diamond and as graphite. In its amorphous or non-crystalline state it occurs as lamp-black and other substances.

Diamonds and graphite are both made up entirely of carbon atoms but each has its own unique properties. The reason for this is the crystal lattice, the arrangement of the atoms in the diamond or the graphite crystal. The differences between these two compounds, both in the visual appearance of the crystal and the arrangement of the carbon atoms, can be seen in the illustration on the right.

We can see the effects of this diversity of structure. Diamonds are very hard (10 on the Mohs scale): graphite is soft enough to be used as the lead in pencils. Diamonds are dazzling while graphite is dark and dull. Industrial diamonds are used in saws, drill bits and polishers to cut through the toughest of materials; graphite, at high temperatures, is an effective lubricant.

The greatest distinction is in the structure of the two. In the diamond crystal lattice, each atom is covalently bonded to *four* of its neighbours. To split a diamond, millions of these bonds must be broken. Graphite, however, has planes of bonded atoms arranged in a honeycomb structure. These planes, separated from each other, easily sheer apart.

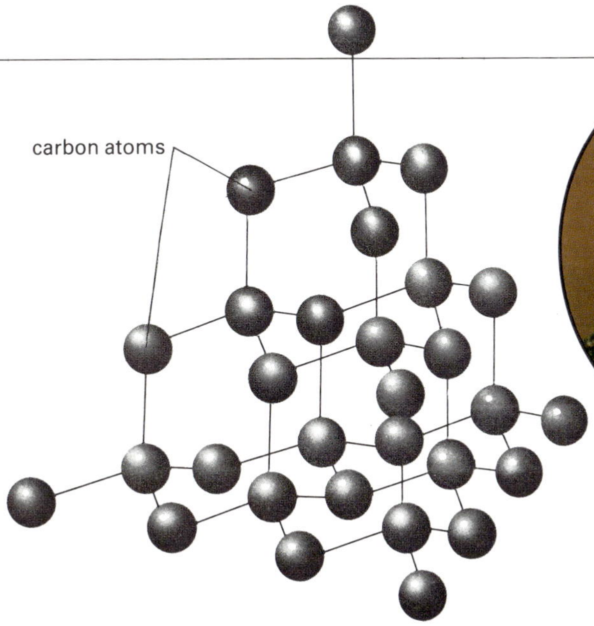

carbon atoms

diamond

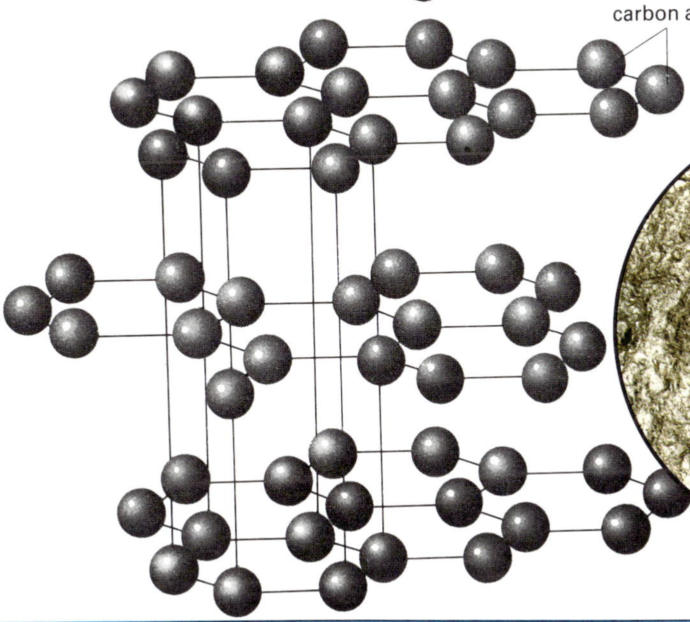

carbon atoms

graphite

ECCENTRIC SOLIDS

Atoms of liquids and gases are not arranged in any coherent order: they are shapeless and amorphous. Strangely enough, there are amorphous solids – those that lack crystalline structure.

The opal, its milky surface shot through with iridescent colours, is one such solid. It is an amorphous form of silica which contains a percentage of water. Glass is stranger still. If the thickness of an old pane of glass is measured top and bottom, we find that the lower half is thicker than the top. The glass has actually flowed downwards, because the silicate materials that are used in its manufacture are in a flexible chain, rather than in a rigid lattice.

Glass is normally classified as a solid, but the flow phenomenon has led some scientists to regard it as a liquid. It is one of the many areas of science where it is difficult to say who is right and who is wrong.

There are other solids, all of them rare elements, which in the pure state actually collapse under the weight of their own crystalline structure.

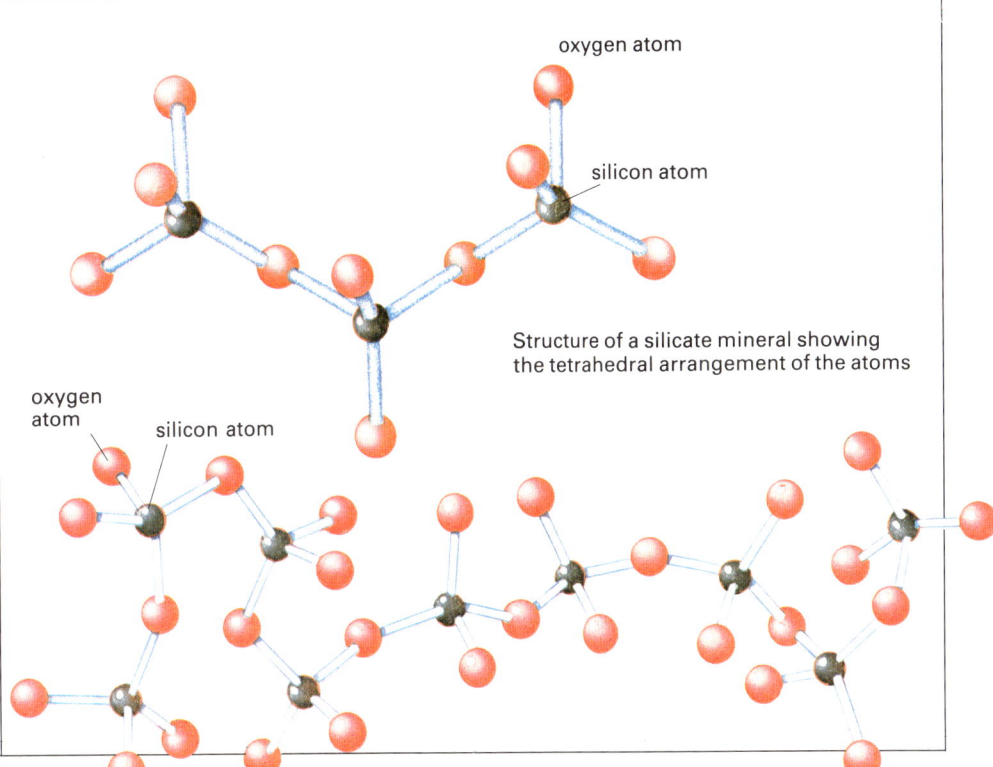

oxygen atom

silicon atom

Structure of a silicate mineral showing the tetrahedral arrangement of the atoms

oxygen atom

silicon atom

16

THE STUDY OF SYMMETRY

We saw earlier that the Earth's surface is made up of three types of rock – igneous, sedimentary and metamorphic. Different minerals are found in the different types of rock; calcite and celestite may be found in sedimentary rocks and gold and copper in metamorphic rocks, for example.

The first man to study crystals and minerals extensively by scientific methods was W. Pryce, an eighteenth-century Cornish vicar, whose work was continued by a Frenchman (curiously enough, also a clergyman), l'Abbé René Just Haüy, whose work led to mineralogy becoming a precise science. His definitions of the seven crystal systems are still in use today. The seven systems are:

Monoclinic: the most common system, about 50% of minerals having monoclinic crystals.
Orthorhombic: about a quarter of minerals have orthorhombic crystals.
Triclinic: about 15% have this structure.
Cubic: less common than triclinic. Apart from the cubic structure there are the derived cubic forms of octahedron and rhombic dodecahedron (a solid with twelve rhombic faces).
Tetragonal: one of the rarer crystal systems.
Hexagonal: the rarest of crystal systems.
Trigonal: closely related to hexagonal crystals and often grouped with them.

AN IMPORTANT CRYSTAL

One particular mineral played an important part in the study of minerals; natural crystalline calcium carbonate, better known as calcite or calcspar.

It occurs in a variety of forms – flat or pointed rhombohedrons, hexagonal bipyramids and hexagonal prisms, which are often found combined at the same spot. Despite the multiplicity of forms, the different shapes all have the same chemical composition, and it was discovered that a sharp impact always produced rhombohedrons with constant angles. It was this fact that led Pryce and Haüy to investigate crystalline structures.

In its pure form, calcite is colourless but it generally occurs as white or pink in colour. It is sometimes pale yellow or yellowish brown and is found in sedimentary rocks.

A general importance

It is difficult to underestimate the importance of minerals to mankind. Some scientists would go so far as to say that all of human industry is based on them. Prehistoric man used minerals to create fire, and to manufacture tools and weapons. Metals are made from them and the cement industry depends on them.

And on a different level, they give us a great deal of pleasure, their physical properties being exploited as they are by the jewel industry.

Igneous rock Formed from the molten material beneath Earth's crust. Examples are basalt and granite.

Sedimentary rock Formed from sedimentary deposits resulting from erosion of the Earth's crust. Examples are limestone, sandstone and clay.

Metamorphic rock Sedimentary or igneous r[ock] modified by high temperatu[re] or pressures – usually both. [Ex]amples are marble and slate.

Below: the illustrations (left) show the different types of rock of which the Earth's crust is composed. The diagrams show the basic crystal structures and their characteristics. A few examples of minerals with these crystal systems are:
monoclinic – gypsum, orthoclase;
triclinic – axinite, albite;
trigonal – quartz, dolomite, silver nitrate;
orthorhombic – topaz, chalcocite;
tetragonal – cassiterite, wulfenite;
hexagonal – calcite, apatite, beryl;
cubic – diamond, fluorite.

GROWING CRYSTALS

It is interesting and quite easy to observe crystal formation. One simple way is to make a sugar solution from sugar and water, and pour it into a saucer. As the water evaporates, small, imperfect crystals will form.

Perfect crystals can be made by making a saturated salt solution, which is poured into a jar and left. Crystals will form. The best should be taken out and have threads tied round them. These can then be suspended in a new saturated solution and the little crystals will continue to grow.

The formation of crystals is favoured by gradual transition from liquid to solid state. This encourages the molecules to form themselves into polyhedra – solid figures with four or more faces which are all polygons.

It is possible to make crystals of most minerals, but there are a few, such as opal, which do not have crystals. These are said to be amorphous. Others may appear to be amorphous, but contain tiny crystals that can only be seen under the microscope. Such minerals are said to be crypto-crystals.

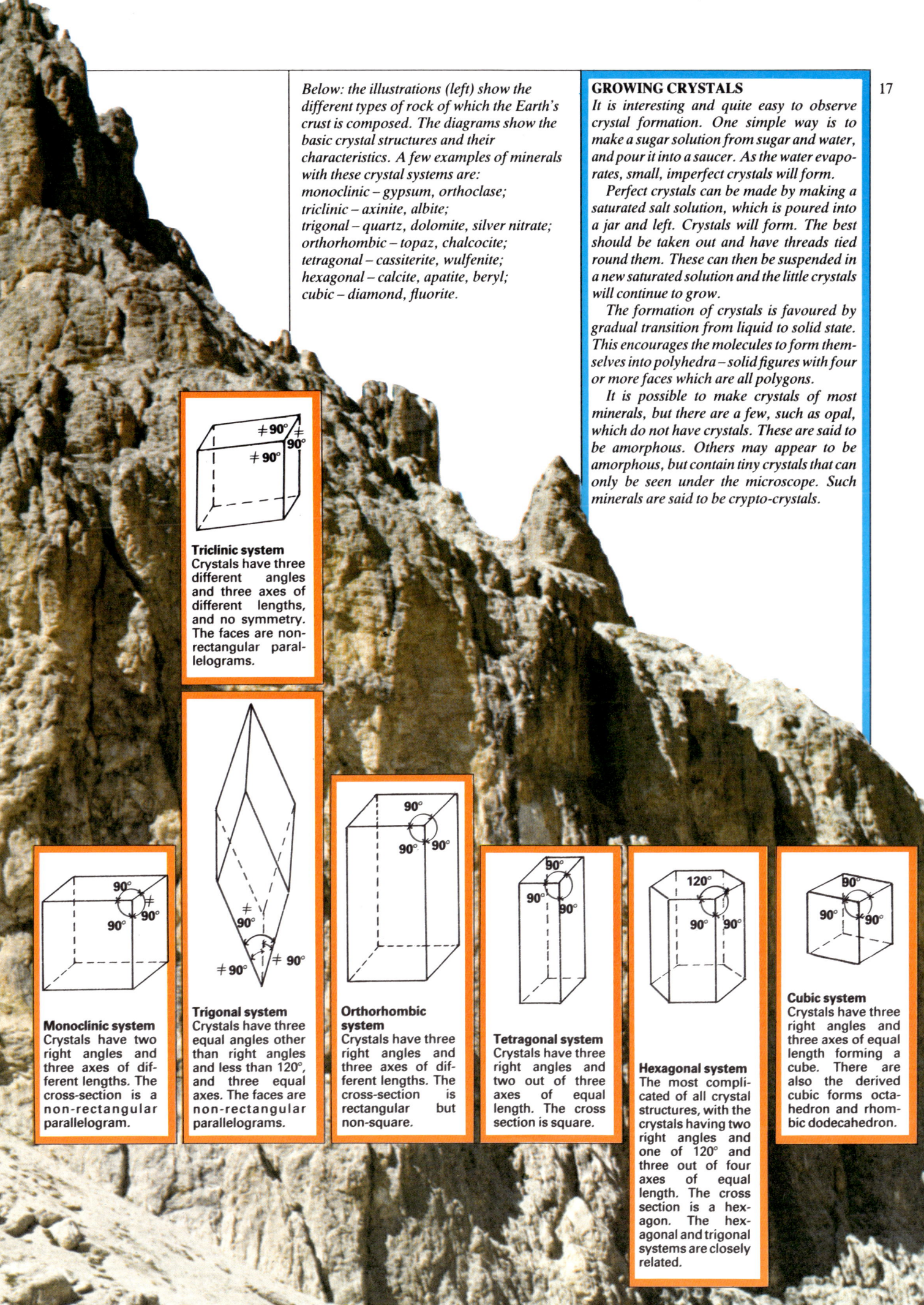

Triclinic system
Crystals have three different angles and three axes of different lengths, and no symmetry. The faces are non-rectangular parallelograms.

Monoclinic system
Crystals have two right angles and three axes of different lengths. The cross-section is a non-rectangular parallelogram.

Trigonal system
Crystals have three equal angles other than right angles and less than 120°, and three equal axes. The faces are non-rectangular parallelograms.

Orthorhombic system
Crystals have three right angles and three axes of different lengths. The cross-section is rectangular but non-square.

Tetragonal system
Crystals have three right angles and two out of three axes of equal length. The cross section is square.

Hexagonal system
The most complicated of all crystal structures, with the crystals having two right angles and one of 120° and three out of four axes of equal length. The cross section is a hexagon. The hexagonal and trigonal systems are closely related.

Cubic system
Crystals have three right angles and three axes of equal length forming a cube. There are also the derived cubic forms octahedron and rhombic dodecahedron.

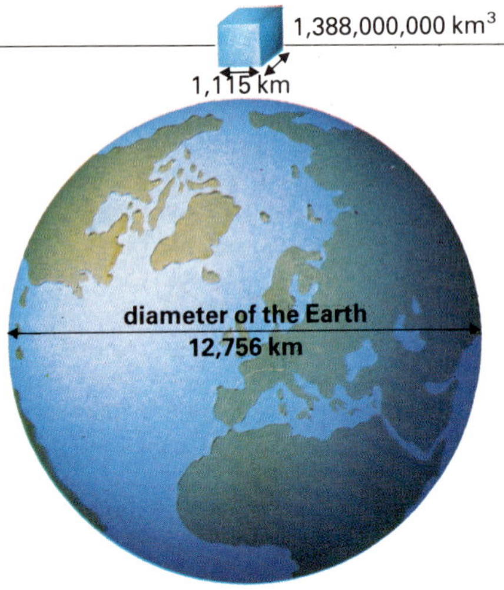

1,388,000,000 km³

1,115 km

biosphere 600 km³

atmosphere 13,000 km³

lake and rivers 200,000 km³

diameter of the Earth
12,756 km

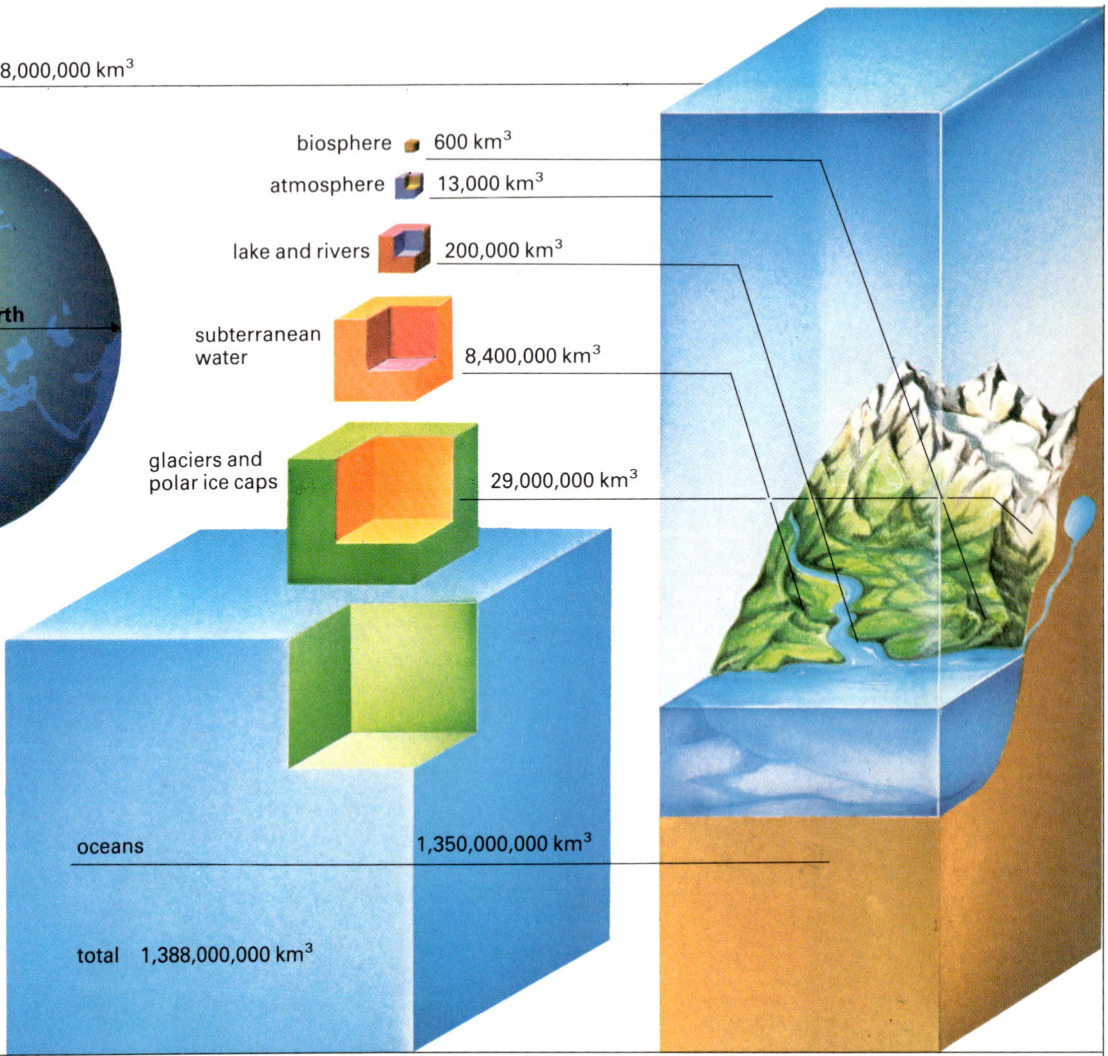

subterranean
water 8,400,000 km³

glaciers and
polar ice caps 29,000,000 km³

Right: these diagrams show just how prominent water is on or beneath the surface of our planet. The oceans alone account for 97·2% of this water content. Below: water, too, is an important constituent of all living organisms, whether animal or vegetable.

oceans 1,350,000,000 km³

total 1,388,000,000 km³

Liquids

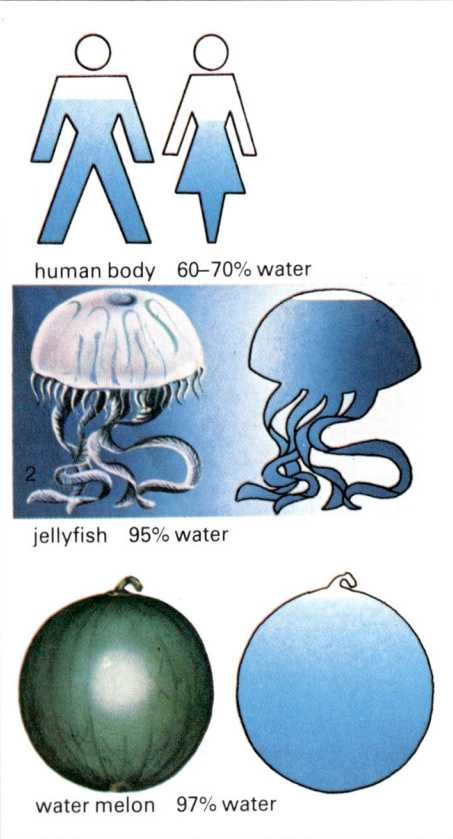

human body 60–70% water

jellyfish 95% water

water melon 97% water

Water is the most important of all liquids. Two-thirds of our bodies is water – other living things have an even higher water content than that. Jellyfish are 95% water and water melons 97%. Without water there would be no life on Earth; many of the chemical reactions on which life depends take place in water. Fortunately for us, there is plenty of it – about 1,390 million cubic kilometres, which if it was in the shape of a cube would have sides measuring 1,115 kilometres each. We use water to drink, to create energy by generating electricity, to help to ensure that our crops mature and ripen. Without water, we would not be here. The western world has been horrified by harrowing scenes of the effect of drought in many parts of Africa. Without rain, plants cannot flourish and without plants, man cannot survive.

THE LIQUID STATE

Liquids have no shape of their own; they adopt the shape of the vessels in which they are contained. In the liquid state, molecules are free to change position relative to their neighbours. Liquids can flow and they can also evaporate as molecules break away and are dissipated into the surrounding air. But liquid is matter and even in this versatile state is governed by well-defined laws. Forces of attraction are still at work between the molecules of a liquid substance. If some oil is dropped into a bowl of water, the two liquids separate and the oil floats to the surface to form a continuous layer.

As we said earlier, all matter can exist as a solid, liquid or gas. Although a block of ice seems worlds apart from the boiling water that spouts from a geyser, there is only one difference between them – the energy level. The lower, vibrational energy of solids is produced by the oscillations of the fixed, tightly bonded molecules. The higher kinetic energy of liquids is the result of the free movement of these molecules.

When the kinetic energy of a liquid is increased by heating, the molecules are released from the force that holds them together and the liquid becomes a vapour.

TRAVELLING THROUGH MATTER

If, by some miracle, we could take a journey through matter in some miniature form, as depicted below, we would find that solids, liquids and gases may all be present at a particular temperature. Inside the flask are a salt crystal, a drop of water and, of course, air. But if all three were converted to the liquid state they would all have different energy levels. In order to melt, the salt would need to be heated; and to liquefy, the air would need to be cooled considerably.

If we could look at the activity of the molecules in greater detail, we would see that the oxygen and nitrogen molecules in the air are free to move about in random fashion separate from each other.

When we reached the drop of water we would find that the molecules behave in a much more orderly fashion. They can still move about, but they cannot separate from each other. And when we finally reach the salt crystal we find a fixed, regular arrangement of chlorine and sodium atoms bonded together in a well-constructed fashion.

The cohesive force binding the water molecules together can be overcome. If a drop of water is left on a glass dish, it will evaporate, some of the molecules moving up into the air. At lower temperatures the cohesive forces in the water are greater than at higher temperatures, when evaporation occurs more quickly. When boiling point is reached, the water molecules have absorbed enough kinetic energy to overcome the cohesive force altogether.

If we pour some water into a graduated cylinder and heat it, the water-level moves up. The heat makes the molecules move more vigorously, striking each other with more energy. The volume of the liquid increases – it expands.

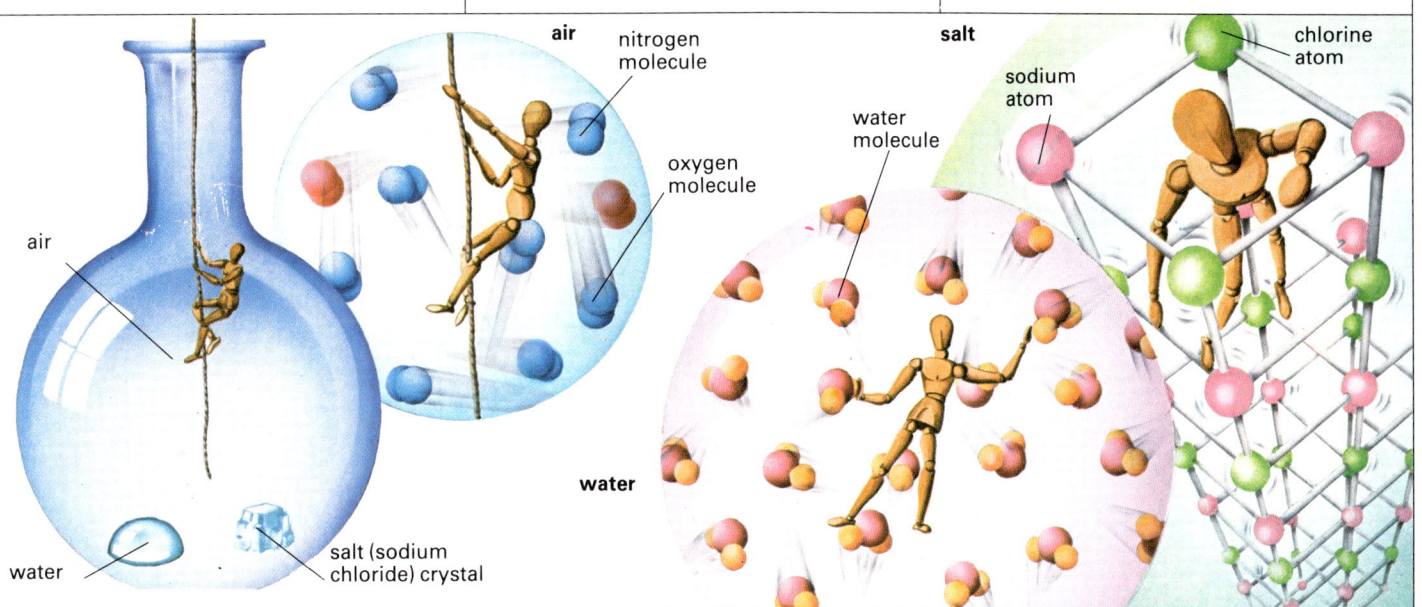

air · nitrogen molecule · oxygen molecule · water · air · water · salt (sodium chloride) crystal · salt · water molecule · sodium atom · chlorine atom

CHANGING STATES

For many solids, such as iron, the melting process is highly dramatic, because it takes place at very high temperatures – about 1,500° C (2,732° F). The metal glows red, then white hot, until finally it has overcome the bonds holding the crystals of iron together, having absorbed enough energy to do so. The molten iron vaporises at 2,800° C (5,072° F). The iron has changed state, from solid to liquid to gas, in the same way that water does, but the energy level required is far greater.

The kinetic energy of liquids is always greater than the vibrational energy of solids. As the iron is heated, energy is absorbed, molecular activity increases and the temperature rises. When the iron reaches melting point, however, the temperature levels out and remains the same, even though heat is still being applied. The temperature begins to rise again once all the metal is molten.

The heat absorbed during the melting process is called latent (literally hidden) heat. The energy is used to change the state of iron from solid to liquid, instead of being used to change the temperature. The latent heat required for melting is called the latent heat of fusion. When a liquid turns to vapour, the energy required for the transformation is called the latent heat of vaporisation.

The amount of energy needed by any pure substance to change state without changing temperature – the specific latent heat – is always constant for the same mass.

If a liquid is allowed to evaporate, its temperature drops. The more active molecules (those with more kinetic energy) break away from the liquid so the average kinetic energy of the remaining liquid is reduced. This is why a rapidly evaporating liquid like surgical spirit feels cold when dabbed on the skin.

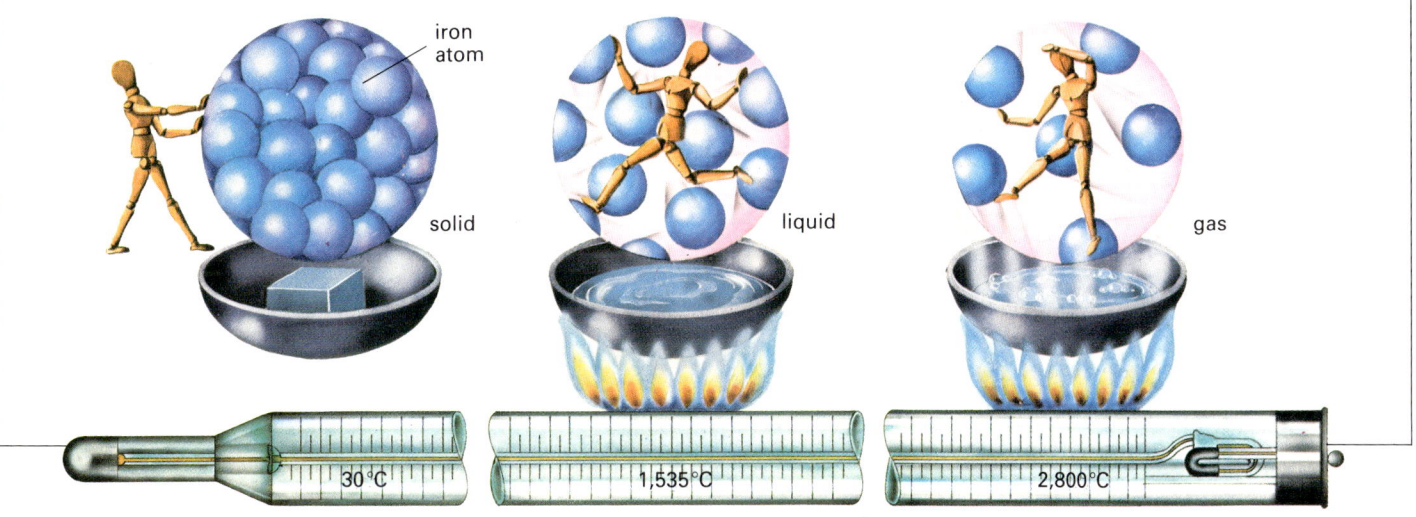

iron atom · solid · liquid · gas · 30°C · 1,535°C · 2,800°C

WALKING ON WATER!

Many children are surprised the first time that they see a pond-skater, because these spindly-legged insects look as if they are walking on the surface of the water. It can't be true, they think, nothing can walk on water. But, in fact, the pond-skater, and similar insects with unwettable feet, can.

It can do so because at the surface of the water the molecules behave slightly differently than they do beneath the surface where every molecule is attracted by those around it. At the surface, there are no upward forces to balance the downward ones because there are no molecules of water above the surface. As a result a surface molecule tends to be pulled into the liquid. The number of molecules at the surface is the smallest possible and the surface behaves as if it had a skin on it. This phenomenon is known as 'surface tension' and when the little pond-skater walks across the surface it is supported by this tension. The weight of the insect actually dents the surface, as if it were rubber!

It is surface tension that enables a needle to float on the surface of water. This can be easily seen if a needle is placed on a piece of absorbent paper and they are both laid on the surface of water. The paper soon becomes saturated and sinks to the bottom. The size and density of the needle does not disturb the surface tension, hence it remains on the surface.

An old theory disproved

The phenomenon of surface tension proves false the old belief that water cannot move upwards without being pumped. It can. This is due to capillarity – the attraction of the molecules of the liquid for each other or for the solid surface with which the water is in contact. If water is enclosed in a narrow glass tube, the attraction between the molecules of water is less than that between it and the glass walls of the tube. This causes the water to run up the surface of the glass.

Another more common manifestation of this is the way in which a sugar lump soaks up a drop of water on which it is placed. The space between the granules of sugar has a similar effect as the glass tube, and the water 'climbs' through the cube and continues to do so until the cube is saturated.

If a capillary tube is immersed in water, the water climbs up inside it; the deeper the tube is immersed the higher up the water climbs. The height to which the water rises is also influenced by the diameter of the tube, being inversely proportional to the diameter of the tube; the narrower the diameter, the higher the elevation. In a tube only one fifth of a millimetre in diameter, water will rise about 15 centimetres. This correlation between the height and the diameter of a tube was established by an English scientist, James Jurin (1684–1750).

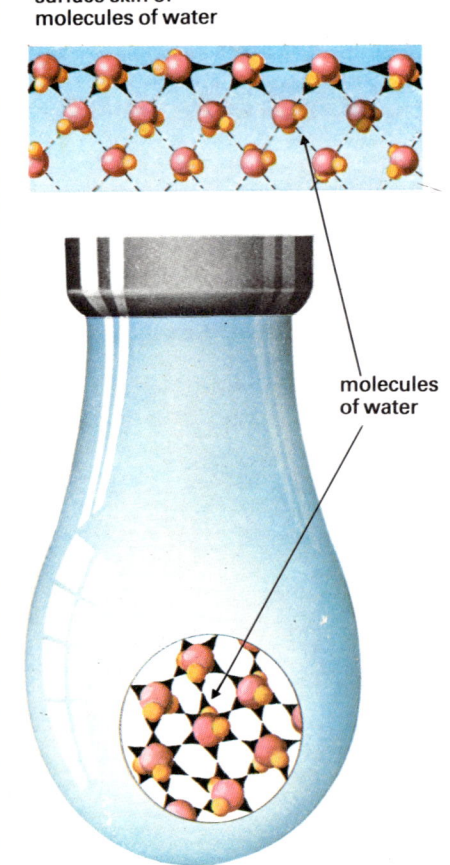

surface skin of
molecules of water

molecules
of water

Breaking the surface tension

Surface tension accounts for the characteristic shape of a drop of water. The attraction between the molecules results in the spherical shape as the 'skin' effect caused by the inward-acting forces holds the bulk of the liquid back. The sphere is distorted because gravitational forces are also acting on it.

But we can break the tension quite easily. Returning for a moment to the little pond-skater below; it now looks as if it is about to sink. Why is the surface tension no longer able to support it? The answer is simple. Someone has added detergent to the water. The detergent molecules interfere with the forces that bind the molecules of water together, thus disrupting the surface tension. In effect, the detergent molecules replace the water molecules at the surface. Detergents and soaps are said to be tensio-active and it is because of their tensio-active properties that we use them to wash ourselves, and our clothes and dishes.

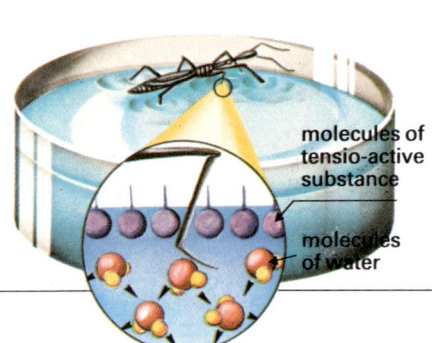

molecules of
tensio-active
substance

molecules
of water

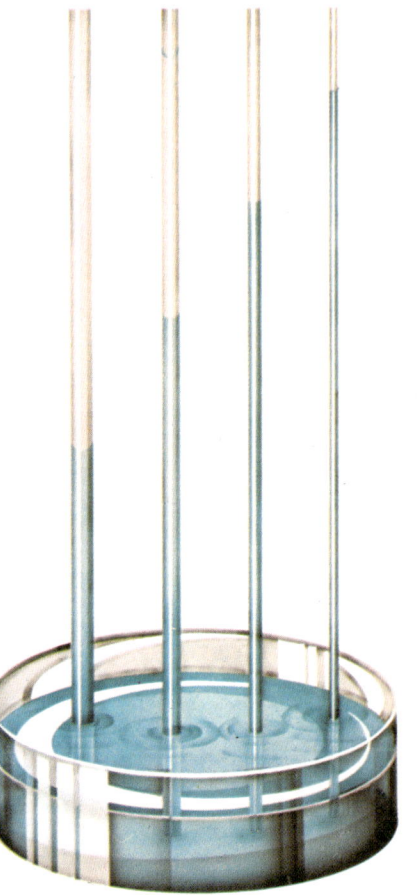

LIQUIDS AND PRESSURE

Liquids have the ability to transmit pressure applied at one point and apply it with equal force in all directions, rather than absorb it at one point. This is why hydraulic pressure can raise a heavy object in one place when a small force is exerted at the other.

Picture for a moment a bus with standing room only; the passengers are treading on each other's toes (above right). The pressure being applied is absorbed at one point, causing pain. The strength of the pressure is dependent on two factors, the force, or weight, behind it, and the area over which it is being applied. On the bus, the person experiencing the most pain is the unfortunate man being trodden on by the woman wearing high-heeled shoes and weighing 100 kilograms. In the hydraulic press (right) the pressure being applied is uniform with the pressure being exerted, but because the area over which it is being exerted is much larger than the area where it is applied, it is transformed into a considerable force.

The same principle can be seen in the hydraulic brake system. The pressure applied on the brake pedal is distributed equally to all four brake shoes, and the car comes to a perfectly balanced halt.

Below: a cubic decimetre made up of 40 iron plates weighs 8 kg and displaces 1 kg of water. It is so dense that it sinks. If a container is made out of the plates it will still weigh 8 kg, but because its volume is increased 16 times its density is decreased and it is able to float.

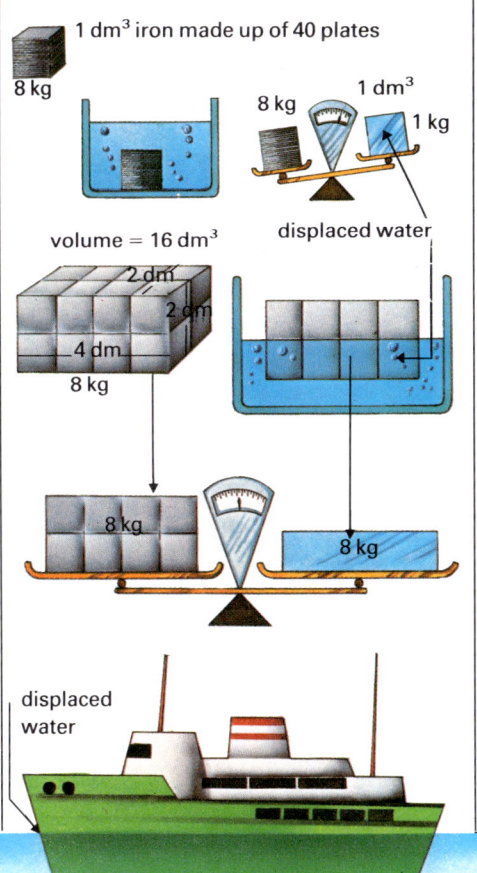

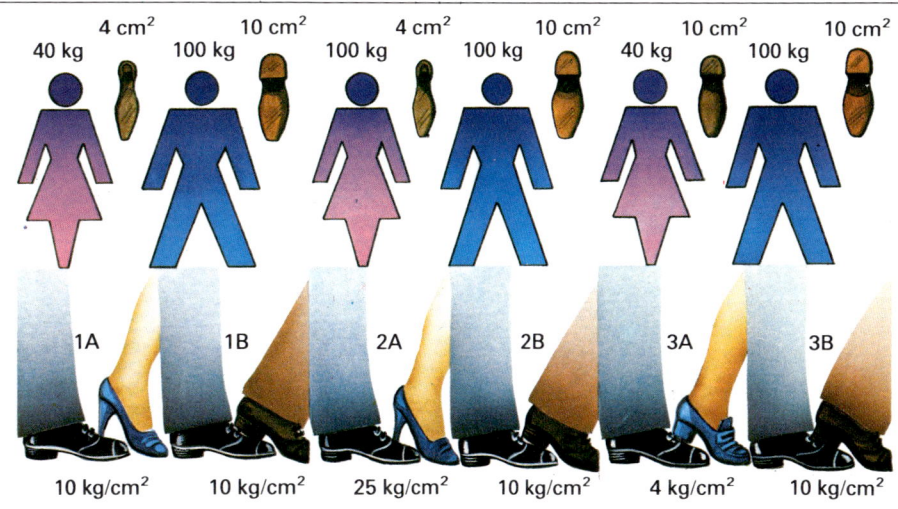

Despite their differences in weight, 1A and 1B exert the same pressure on the toes on which they are standing. 40 kg exerted over 4 cm^2 gives the same value as 100 kg over 10 cm^2 – 10 km/cm^2. 2A and 2B are the same weight, but because the area on which the pressure is exerted is smaller, the woman's heel exerts 25 kg/cm^2, whereas the man produces only 10 kg/cm^2 because his weight is spread over a wider area. Couple 3A and 3B are wearing shoes with the same heel area, but because of the differences in weight the pressure exerted by the man is more than that produced by the woman.

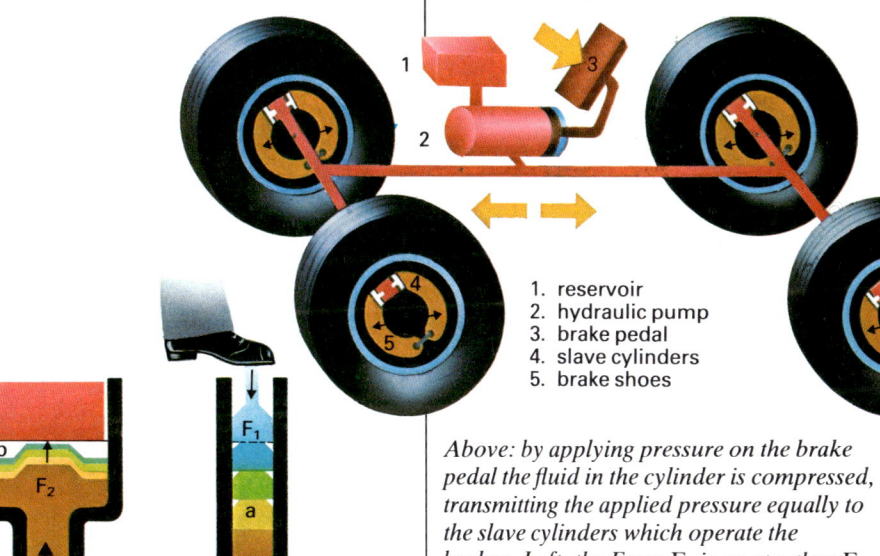

1. reservoir
2. hydraulic pump
3. brake pedal
4. slave cylinders
5. brake shoes

Above: by applying pressure on the brake pedal the fluid in the cylinder is compressed, transmitting the applied pressure equally to the slave cylinders which operate the brakes. Left: the Force F$_2$ is greater than F$_1$ because the pressure is transmitted from a small area, a, to a larger one, b.

WHY DOES A SHIP FLOAT?

If a piece of metal is thrown into the water, it sinks. If a piece of wood is thrown in, it floats. To say that the metal sinks because it is heavier than the wood is not quite true; what do we mean by heavier?

If we took equal volumes of water, wood and iron – say one cubic decimetre – and weighed them, we would find that the water weighed 1 kg, the wood 0·8 kg and the iron 8 kg. So an equal volume of water is heavier than wood but lighter than metal. The mass per unit of volume of a substance is called its density. The larger the volume over which a weight is dispersed, the less its density will be, and if the density of a body is less than that of water it will float. As it does so, it displaces an equal weight of water.

The founding father of this principle was a Greek philosopher, Archimedes, who stated that when a body is totally or partially immersed in water it experiences an upthrust equal to the weight of the fluid displaced. This led to the principle of flotation: the apparent loss of weight of a body immersed in a fluid is equal to the weight of fluid displaced. When the container weighing 8 kg displaces 8 kg of water, half of it, weighing 4 kg, is still above the water with an equal weight beneath. At this point it experiences an upthrust of 8 kg, equal to the weight of water displaced, and therefore it floats.

The same principle keeps the ship in the illustration alongside floating on the water.

This extraordinary machine, which is still at the design stage, could have a brilliant future in the mining industry if it ever gets off the drawing board; it could do the work of ten men. High-pressure water jets are aimed at the coal seam, loosening chunks of it and causing them to fall into the skip at the front of the contraption. They are then pulverised by a grinding machine. The grit is then mixed with water and pumped to the back and up to the surface. The remote-controlled robot could well revolutionise the way in which we dig out one of the most important of all minerals.

AN OLD SOURCE OF ENERGY

Coal, one of the first fuels to be used by man, has declined in importance over the last century or so; we have come to rely increasingly on oil and natural gas to provide the energy that we need to power our industries and heat our homes. Gas and oil are more manageable; they are comparatively easily pumped and transported from source to consumer.

Coal, on the other hand, is difficult to get at, cumbersome to carry to the surface and has to be carried from pithead to customer by road or rail.

Pits have closed as accessible coal seams run out and it becomes harder and harder to make mining the coal worth while. Miners in the coalfields of Europe and America are facing increasingly difficult times.

But the world's oil and natural gas resources are being used up very rapidly. Britain's North Sea oil fields on which so much hope was pinned are estimated to run dry by the second decade of the next century. There is, however, abundant coal under the surface of the Earth – enough to meet the world's energy demands for the next three or four hundred years.

Little by little, coal is regaining its old importance. Modern mining technology can make once unworkable seams accessible and economic to exploit. New transport methods will make transportation easier and new geological survey techniques make it very likely that new sources of coal will be discovered. 'King Coal,' one commentator has observed, 'never died. He merely went into exile and waited to be recalled.'

Coal

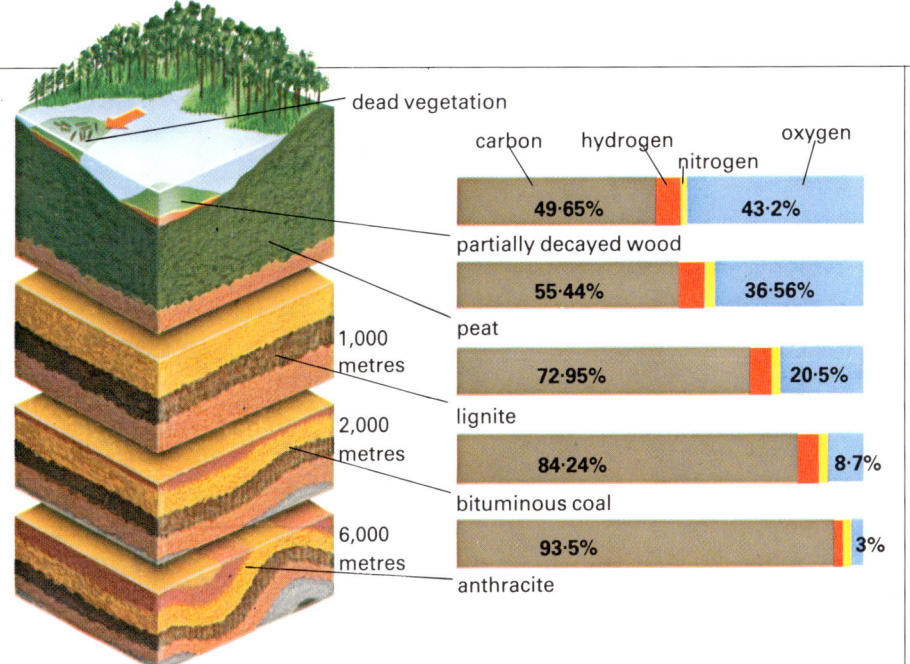

dead vegetation

	carbon	hydrogen	nitrogen	oxygen
partially decayed wood	49·65%			43·2%
peat	55·44%			36·56%
lignite	72·95%			20·5%
bituminous coal	84·24%			8·7%
anthracite	93·5%			3%

1,000 metres

2,000 metres

6,000 metres

Left: dead trees and other vegetable matter collect in a mass and sink. This begins to decay and becomes buried under layers of sediment and more dead vegetation, forming peat and eventually coal of various types. The different levels at which the different types of coal are found can be seen in this diagram; peat, for example, being near the surface and subject to little pressure, is soft and spongy. As we go deeper, the pressure increases and the different grades of coal are formed. Also shown is the chemical content of each type, the quality of the coal being determined by the proportions of carbon, hydrogen, oxygen and nitrogen. The higher the carbon content the more difficult the coal is to light, but the more efficient it is.

Right: four types of coal with different characteristics and different energy potentials, including partially decayed wood which is the first stage in the formation of coal. Cannel coal is a sub-bituminous coal formed from completely rotten vegetation, rather than partially decayed which forms peat.

A FOSSIL FUEL

Coal is a fossil fuel. It is formed by the pressure that built up on top of the mighty forests of the Carboniferous Period which became buried 300 million years ago, providing us with a store of energy to be used today. The dead vegetation, buried in fresh-water swamps by layers of sediment and more vegetation, became preserved in a partially decayed form and changed into peat. As pressure and heat built up, the peat became lignite (brown coal), then bituminous – soft – coal, and finally the hard coal called anthracite.

The energy in coal is solar energy. Plants perform photosynthesis which uses the energy of the Sun to manufacture their food. It is this store of solar energy in prehistoric vegetation that gives coal *its* energy.

All plants are composed of carbon, hydrogen and oxygen. Heat and pressure gradually reduce the hydrogen and oxygen content. The longer the coal is underground and the deeper it lies, the higher its carbon content and hence its energy potential. In extreme cases, the pressure is so intense that pure carbon – graphite – results. Switzerland has substantial graphite deposits.

Oil, another carbon-based fuel, was formed by a similar process involving vegetable and animal debris which developed into a thick ooze. This was turned, by pressure, into oil-bearing lime- and sandstone. But whereas the hydrogen and oxygen has been squeezed out of coal, oil is a mixture of carbon and hydrogen compounds. It must be refined before it can be used.

anthracite

cannel coal

partially decayed wood

lignite

GENERATING POWER

The power station illustrated below is one in which the basic fuel is coal. Electricity is also generated using oil, water, natural gas or nuclear fission, and other less used sources of electric power are the Sun, winds and tides, and geothermal energy.

The process takes place in three main areas – in the boiler (A), in the steam turbine (B) and in the generator (C). Coal is brought in by a conveyor belt (1) and fed into a hopper (2). It is pulverised in a grinding mill (3) and the dust is mixed with warmed air from the air intake and blown into the furnace (4), where it is mixed with the remainder of the warmed combustion air. The mixture burns readily, heating water circulating in the pipes (5) to produce steam. The hot exhaust gases from the combustion chamber are used to reheat circulating steam and to warm the combustion air in the preheater (6). The exhaust gases are then cleaned and released into the atmosphere through the chimney (7). The steam produced is released, when hot enough, to the turbine (B) where it is used three times in order to extract maximum energy from it. At its highest pressure (8) it drives the first stage of turbine blades, and is then recirculated for reheating (9) by the hot exhaust gases from the combustion chamber. It then returns (10) to drive the next stage of blades, and finally the last of its power is extracted by a stage of much longer blades. The exhaust steam passes into a heat exchanger (11) and is condensed, and the water pumped back (12) to begin the whole process again. The heated water from the heat exchanger is recycled through a cooling tower (13). The generator (C) is powered by the steam-driven turbine which drives the shaft (armature) to which electromagnets are attached. These rotate inside the coil windings (14) producing electric current which is fed into the National Grid.

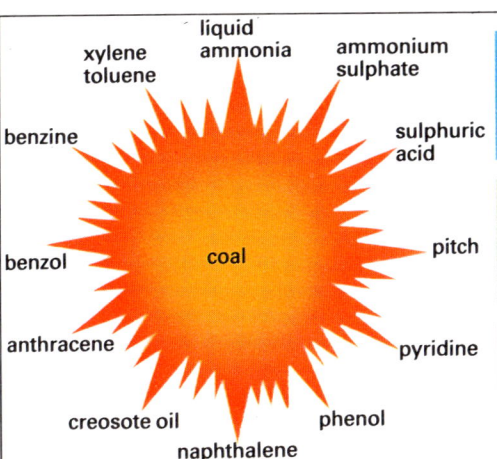

xylene
toluene
liquid ammonia
ammonium sulphate
benzine
sulphuric acid
benzol
coal
pitch
anthracene
pyridine
creosote oil
phenol
naphthalene

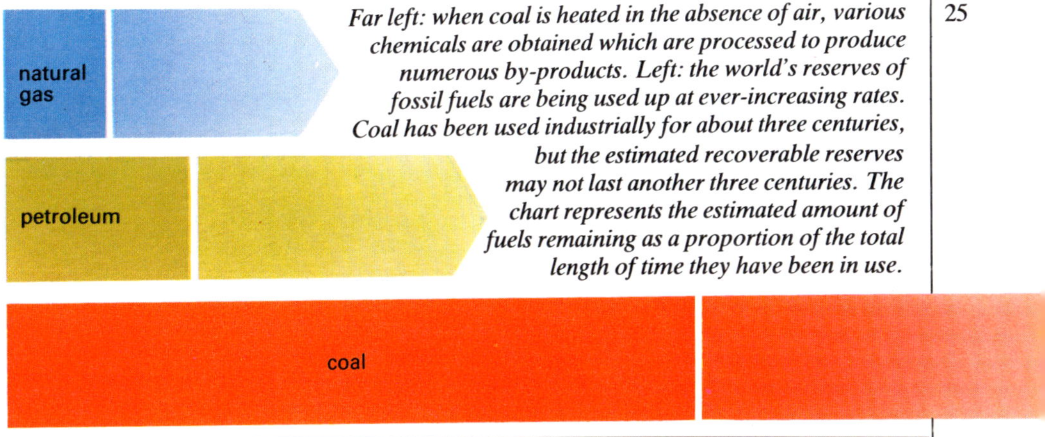

natural gas

petroleum

coal

Far left: when coal is heated in the absence of air, various chemicals are obtained which are processed to produce numerous by-products. Left: the world's reserves of fossil fuels are being used up at ever-increasing rates. Coal has been used industrially for about three centuries, but the estimated recoverable reserves may not last another three centuries. The chart represents the estimated amount of fuels remaining as a proportion of the total length of time they have been in use.

IN THE FUTURE

Coal provides us with an excellent source of efficient fuel and there are stocks of it around the world. So scientists, as well as looking at alternative power supplies, have developed methods of using our coal resources more efficiently.

One new and efficient coal-burning system – called a fluidised bed because it has some of the properties and the appearance of a boiling fluid – has many advantages over other systems. It can use low-grade fuels successfully, in a wide range of sizes of lump or crushed coal; heat loss is cut significantly; smaller and cheaper boilers and furnaces can be used; and atmospheric pollution is considerably reduced.

The coal is burnt in a bed of an incombustible material such as sand, which rests on a distribution plate, through which air is blown upwards at 'fluidising velocity'. This is a speed at which air bubbles are forced through the bed, causing turbulence and a rapid mixing of the particles. Water, preheated by the hot combustion gases, is passed through tubes buried in the bed and is quickly heated to form steam to drive a turbine. The coal is fed in continuously, and the bed is maintained at a temperature which produces a fine ash that moves down through the bed. The sulphur dioxide produced from the burning fuel is prevented from passing into the atmosphere by the addition of lime-stone to the end. This reacts with the sulphur dioxide, producing a solid which is removed with the ash.

The use of a fluidised bed allows the size of the power station to be reduced and approximately 50% of the heat produced is extracted as steam, compared with the 30% of a conventional system. This means that for every ten bags of fuel used, only five are used unproductively, instead of the seven unproductive sacks of the conventional method.

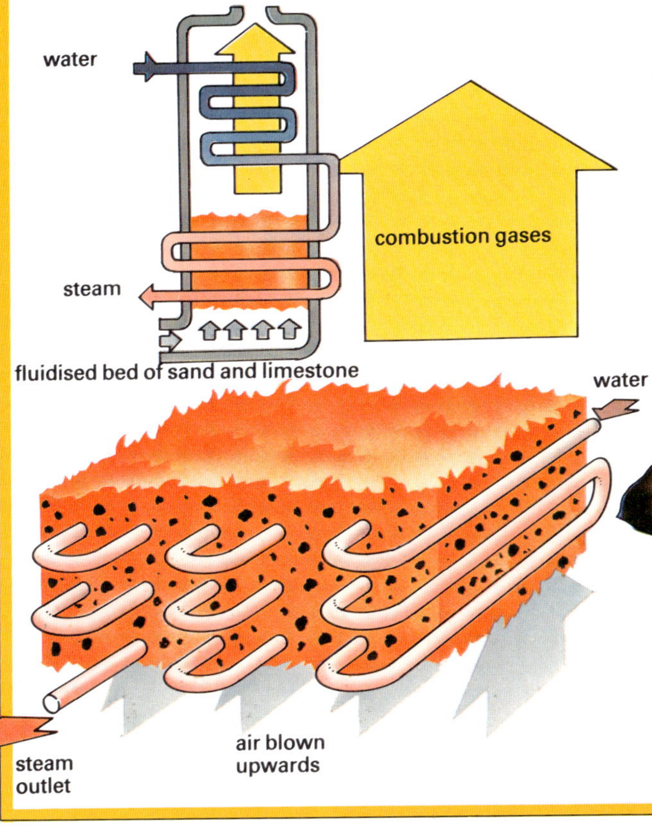

water

steam

combustion gases

fluidised bed of sand and limestone

water

steam outlet

air blown upwards

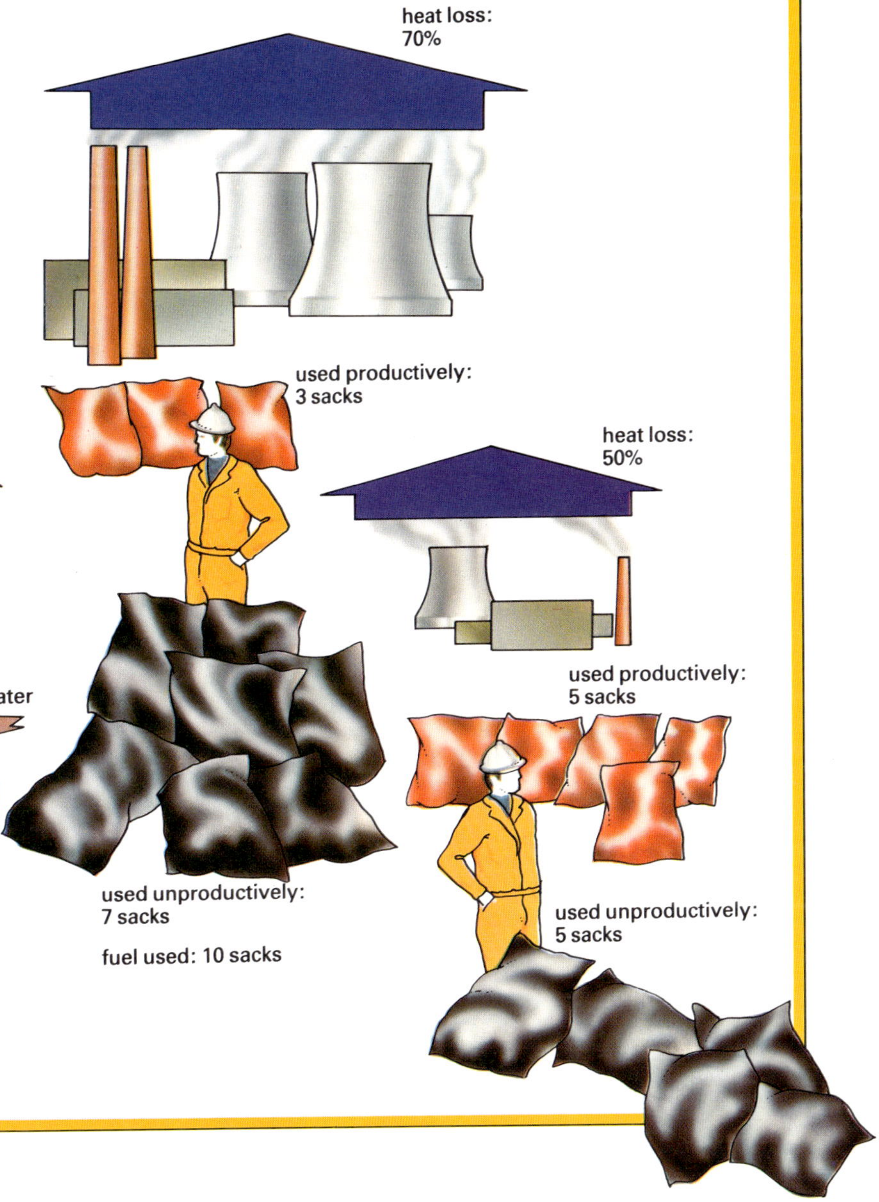

heat loss: 70%

used productively: 3 sacks

used unproductively: 7 sacks

fuel used: 10 sacks

heat loss: 50%

used productively: 5 sacks

used unproductively: 5 sacks

Metals and Metalloids

A modern Indonesian silversmith practises his art in a traditional way. Blowing on a flame to heat it up and applying the heat to a piece of silver, he is able to transform a lump of metal from an unwieldy solid to a malleable state that he can then shape to his own design. Man has known since prehistoric times that metals and metalloids (non-metallic elements that have some of the properties of metals) soften when heat is applied to them. This knowledge enabled man to take the enormous jump into the Metal Ages, putting him firmly on the road to civilisation. Metals remain vital to us today . . . several thousands of years later.

ELEMENTS OF VARIOUS TYPES

Every schoolchild knows that iron, copper and aluminium are metals and that oxygen and hydrogen are not, but this distinction is not, unfortunately, always so easy to make.

Many of the elements classified as metals bear little resemblance to the schoolchild's understanding of the word. Given a piece of soft grey stuff that can easily be cut with a knife and is light enough to float on water, an unknowing person would be surprised to learn that it is a metal – sodium – and is classified as such, along with iron and aluminium and the other elements that spring to mind when we think of a metal.

We usually think of metals as being hard substances, the shapes of which can only be changed under pressure, and usually shiny or with a metallic sheen. Scientists add two more conditions that should be fulfilled before an element can be considered as metal. They should be good conductors of heat and of electricity.

The scientific definition of a metal therefore, is a substance which is lustrous and malleable and which conducts heat and electricity. All metals possess these characteristics to varying degrees. Elements that possess only some of them are termed semi-metals or metalloids, and those that do not possess any are called non-metals. Most metals are also ductile – they can be drawn into a wire. The elements classified as metals vary very much in their properties. They also vary in their melting points, from 70°–3,370° C. Many metals in their pure state are unsuitable for practical uses, but by mixing two or more together, alloys can be produced which have a wide range of special properties and uses.

METALS AS CONDUCTORS

As we have just seen, two of the criteria on which scientists decide whether or not an element is a metal or a non-metal is its ability to conduct heat and electricity.

The atoms of all metallic elements are bonded in such a way that they release one or more electrons and thus acquire a positive charge. The electrons, free from their attachment to the atom, can flow in an electric field, thus giving the metals their ability to conduct electricity. Many buildings have metallic strips running down from the roof to the ground. These attract any lightning flashes and conduct the electricity to where it can be safely earthed.

The atoms of metals also allow heat energy to pass through them without themselves perceptibly moving, which is why they are used so widely in the manufacture of kettles and saucepans. Copper is a particularly good heat conductor (silver is better, but is much more expensive) which is why copper-based saucepans are so effective.

Non-metals, poor conductors, also have their uses. Because they do not conduct heat well, they are good insulators. Heat trapped in a room that is well insulated finds it difficult to escape and thus the temperature is maintained. Conversely, heat can be kept out of a well-insulated room if a low temperature is desired.

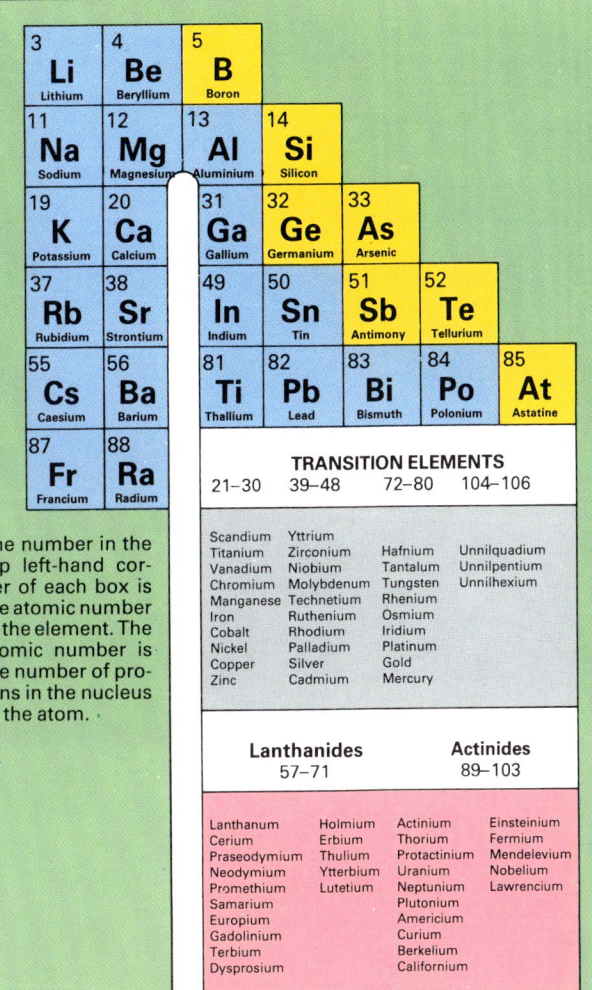

The number in the top left-hand corner of each box is the atomic number of the element. The atomic number is the number of protons in the nucleus of the atom.

TRANSITION ELEMENTS
21–30 39–48 72–80 104–106

Scandium   Yttrium
Titanium   Zirconium   Hafnium   Unnilquadium
Vanadium   Niobium   Tantalum   Unnilpentium
Chromium   Molybdenum   Tungsten   Unnilhexium
Manganese   Technetium   Rhenium
Iron   Ruthenium   Osmium
Cobalt   Rhodium   Iridium
Nickel   Palladium   Platinum
Copper   Silver   Gold
Zinc   Cadmium   Mercury

Lanthanides   Actinides
57–71   89–103

Lanthanum   Holmium   Actinium   Einsteinium
Cerium   Erbium   Thorium   Fermium
Praseodymium Thulium   Protactinium Mendelevium
Neodymium   Ytterbium Uranium   Nobelium
Promethium   Lutetium   Neptunium   Lawrencium
Samarium   Plutonium
Europium   Americium
Gadolinium   Curium
Terbium   Berkelium
Dysprosium   Californium

Elements shown in blue are metals; those in yellow have some metallic properties – metalloids. Some of the elements seen in the group of metals are biologically important, like sodium, calcium and potassium. Two of the metalloids, silicon and germanium, are the elements on which the whole transistor industry is based.

The ten elements from scandium to zinc, and those under them in the Periodic Table, are termed the transition elements. They have variable valencies and are able to form compounds of themselves in different states. The compounds and solutions of transition metals are usually coloured. The elements with atomic numbers 104–106 are sometimes included with the lanthanides.

The elements immediately following lanthanium and actinium are often called the inner transition elements. The lanthanides have properties resembling those of aluminium, and the actinides are all radioactive. Both of these groups are important in nuclear technology.

Below: although it is a metal, sodium is easy to cut with a knife. It quickly tarnishes when it comes into contact with air and has to be stored in oil. It cannot be stored in water because it reacts very violently with it. Above: the elements which are metals, and those which are metalloids. The metalloids, or semi-metals, form the border between metals and non-metals.

Shedding electrons

Why are the atoms of metals so willing to shed the electrons and thus give the elements their conductive properties? As in all atoms, the negatively-charged electrons are held in their orbit around the nucleus by the attractions between them and the positively-charged protons in the nucleus. The atoms of most metals are larger than those of non-metals, so the electrons in the outer shell are further away from the nucleus. There is, therefore, less attraction – the larger the atom, the more easy it is for the outer electrons to free themselves.

As well as giving metals the ability to conduct heat and electricity, the ready shedding of the outer electrons accounts for the fact that most metals are able to form compounds naturally with non-metals. More often than not, the compound has little commercial or industrial value, and the metal in it has to be extracted. The method of extraction depends on the metals and the elements to which they are bonded. Copper is extracted from copper sulphide, for example, simply by applying heat at the required temperature, but the aluminium in aluminium oxide has to be extracted by a complicated process of electrolysis.

METALS AND NON-METALS
The Periodic Table places the elements within it in horizontal rows called periods and vertical columns called groups. As one moves across a period there is a general trend from metallic to non-metallic behaviour. The non-metals include such well-known elements as hydrogen, carbon, oxygen, nitrogen, fluorine, phosphorus, sulphur and chlorine. There are also the noble gases such as helium and neon. The elements between the obvious metals and the definite non-metals are the metalloids, such as arsenic and silicon. The remaining elements, 81 in all, are reckoned to be metals. They will combine with oxygen in base solutions to neutralise acids.

Metallurgists subdivide metals into four groups – heavy metals, for example iron, nickel, tin, tungsten, chromium, copper, lead, zinc and gold; aluminium metals, of which aluminium is the most important; the highly reactive alkali metals, lithium, rubidium, caesium, francium, potassium and sodium; and the alkaline-earth metals, radium, strontium, beryllium, calcium, magnesium and barium. The last group form very strong compounds and it is difficult to extract them.

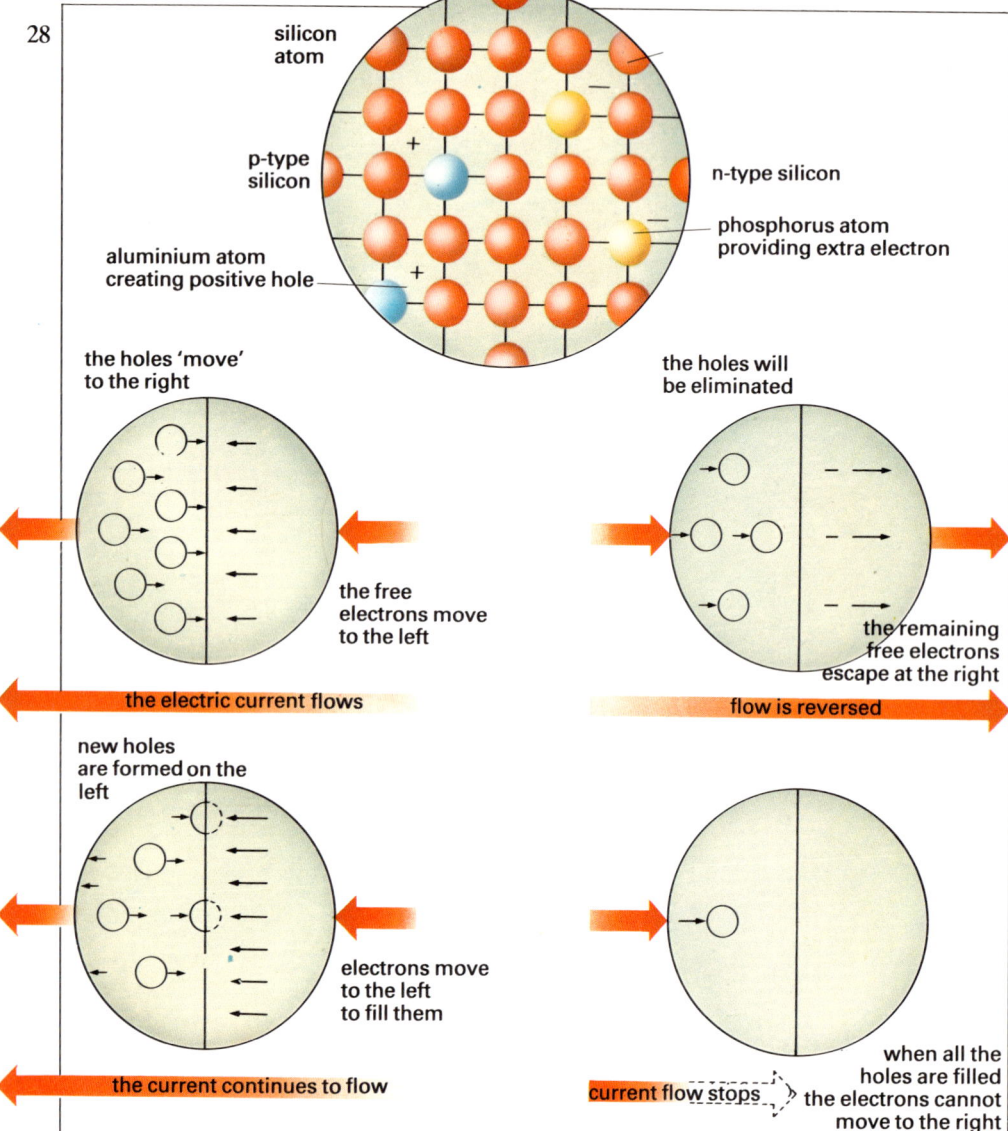

28

silicon atom

p-type silicon

aluminium atom creating positive hole

n-type silicon

phosphorus atom providing extra electron

the holes 'move' to the right

the free electrons move to the left

the electric current flows

new holes are formed on the left

electrons move to the left to fill them

the current continues to flow

the holes will be eliminated

the remaining free electrons escape at the right

flow is reversed

when all the holes are filled the electrons cannot move to the right

current flow stops

TRANSISTORS

When a layer of one type of semiconductor is sandwiched between two layers of the opposite type, a two-junction, three-layer semiconductor device is made, known as a junction transistor. If an n-type is sandwiched between two p-types we have a p-n-p device, and a p-type sandwiched between two n-types produces an n-p-n one. In the latter the two n layers are the collector and the emitter and the p layer, which is doctored to have relatively few holes, is the base. Power is connected so the electrons flow across the base from the emitter to the collector, and a small current must also be fed to the base to neutralise the negative charge which builds up and blocks the flow. The large flow of electrons from emitter to collector, the collector current, is proportional to the small flow of the base current, so the transistor acts as a current amplifier. It can also be used as a high-speed switching device.

Transistors require little electricity to work effectively and can be miniaturised without loss of power. They are the bases on which the important post-war electronics industry has been built.

MERCURY – A LIQUID METAL

This fascinating element, the only metal that is liquid at room temperature, has been known for hundreds of years, and because of its fluid properties and colour was known as quicksilver. The symbol for mercury, Hg, comes from its Latin name, hydrargyrum, meaning liquid silver. It is used in thermometers, scientific apparatus, and amalgams of it are sometimes used in dentistry. If an electric current is passed through it in its vaporised state, the resulting light is rich in ultraviolet radiation and can be used in artificial sun-ray treatment. Mercury vapour lamps are also used for outdoor and street-lighting. It also has a use as an interrupter for breaking an electric circuit. If a small, revolving, air-tight bulb is half-filled with mercury, in which are the terminals of the circuit, it can cut off and reinstate the current. When the bulb turns the current is cut off, but when it returns to its original position, the electrodes are reimmersed in the mercury and the current is restored.

SEMICONDUCTORS

Of the seven 'frontier' elements (those in yellow on the chart on page 27) positioned in the Periodic Table between the metals and the non-metals, two have, over the last 30 years, become of tremendous importance to the electronics industry; indeed, they are the very foundations on which the industry has developed. The two elements are silicon and germanium.

In their natural state these two elements are bad conductors of electricity. The atoms of metals with good conductive qualities readily shed electrons, allowing an electric current to flow through the metal, but the electrons in silicon and germanium atoms are held firmly in the crystal lattice.

Silicon and germanium have a valency of four, which means they have four electrons available for bonding with other atoms. If we add an impurity such as phosphorus or arsenic – elements with a valency of five – four of the electrons of the impurity atom will form bonds with the electrons of four of the other atoms in the crystal lattice, leaving a spare electron. This becomes a free electron, able to move through the lattice. These free electrons carry the electric cur-

rent and are at a higher level of energy than the valency electrons. This higher energy level is called the conduction band.

The amount of impurity that has to be added is tiny; one part in 100,000,000 is sufficient for silicon. The impurity is referred to as a donor impurity, giving as it does an extra electron to the conduction band. The semiconductor thus formed is called an n-type (n standing for the negative charge of the donated electron).

Positive (p-type) semiconductors are made by adding an impurity with a valency of three, such as aluminium or boron to the silicon or germanium. When an atom of aluminium takes the place of an atom of silicon in the lattice, it is only able to form three covalent bonds, so one of the four needed is incomplete. This deficiency of an electron in the valency band is called a hole. Electricity is conducted because the hole is filled by an electron from an adjacent atom, creating a new hole which is immediately filled by another electron. Wherever there is a hole, the total charge of the three remaining electrons is less than the positive charge of the nucleus they surround, so a hole is a positive charge carrier.

MOST USEFUL, MOST ABUNDANT, MOST PRECIOUS AND RAREST . . .

Iron (Fe) occurs in ores all around the world and has been used since prehistoric times to make an enormous variety of things. The iron has to be extracted from the ore, usually by smelting which reduces the oxide to the metal by releasing the carbon gases, and separates out the impurities. The iron produced is then usually used in the manufacture of steel.

It is the second most abundant metal on Earth; aluminium is by far the most common, normally occurring as bauxite – aluminium oxide – which is easily mined. The lightness, strength and attractive lustre of the metal make it a popular metal for use in the manufacture of household goods such as saucepans and kitchen foils.

Gold occurs as a free metal rather than as ore. It has been valued since ancient times for its beauty, and until the early twentieth century was the basis on which currencies were valued. Two-thirds of the world's gold is produced in South Africa. It is easily melted and either cast into bars, which are stored and securely guarded in vaults around the world, or used to manufacture jewellery and precious objets d'art.

The rarest metal on Earth is called unnilhexium. It was produced at a Russian research centre by firing isotopes of oxygen at a target of the element californium. It exists for a fraction of a second, after which it disintegrates as alpha particles.

As we have just seen, two metals that have acquired great significance in recent years are silicon and germanium. The electronics industry is based on their properties of semiconductivity. Without them, it would be impossible to manufacture the powerful computers and tiny calculators that are so important today, also the small portable radios, televisions and cassette players that so many of us use; and we would have been unable to make our historic journeys into space, and to set foot on the Moon.

ALLOYS

Many metals are of little use in their pure state but when combined with others into alloys, strength, hardness and heat resistance can all be improved and the alloy therefore may have much more value than the raw metals. The alloys have different properties from their component metals because of the different atomic structure, and do not normally consist of equal parts of the component metals. Weak metals such as aluminium and copper cannot take much stress, but an alloy of 10% aluminium and 90% copper produces a metal that is as strong as mild steel.

The first alloy which was produced in the world was probably bronze – a mixture of copper and tin – which eventually replaced stone for tools and weapons.

Metals mixed with non-metals

Modern technology has now given us the means of making alloys of metals and non-metals. This has been of tremendous use in nuclear technology. Examples of such alloys are mixtures of metals and ceramics called cermets, which have all the heat conducting abilities of metals and the resistance to corrosion of ceramics, a very useful combination indeed. They are also used in the manufacture of machine tools for shaping metals, as they can stand up to the high temperatures that result from friction.

A metal/non-metal mixture that produces a very hard alloy much in use is a mixture of carbon and tungsten, known as tungsten carbide. This can take one of two forms, WC or W_2C, both being made by heating the two elements together. WC has a very high melting point and will conduct electricity; W_2C has a higher melting point but is a less effective conductor.

An example of the use of a metal/non-metal alloy in the machine-tool industry. Because the tungsten carbide cutting tip can stand greater temperatures, the machine can be turned faster and used for longer periods, being less affected by the high temperatures that result from the extra friction.

Acids and bases are two of the most important chemical substances. They used to be best known for their corrosive properties and were sometimes named after them: nitric acid, for example, was called aqua fortis – strong water – by the medieval alchemist and because a mixture of nitric and hydrochloric acids could dissolve the noble metals, gold and platinum, it was called aqua regia – royal water. We can see some acids and bases, or the effect they can cause, below. On the left, sulphur trioxide reacting with water to become sulphuric acid; on the right a synthetic cloth badly damaged by this strong acid; in the centre, a base, calcium oxide, the very corrosive quicklime. But acids can be beneficial as well as damaging; boric acid, for instance, is used as an antiseptic and to treat certain eye ailments.

ACIDS EVERYWHERE

When we think of acids, most of us think of a corrosive liquid which can eat into cloth, metal – even into flesh and bone – or of chemical laboratories where scientists carefully add small quantities of acids to various substances and note the smoking and bubbling results. In fact we use acids in our everyday lives, and a lot of the foods that we eat contain acids.

Hydrochloric acid, when very concentrated, is a highly toxic substance with a suffocating smell, but it is also one of the many ingredients of ordinary furniture polish. Vinegar contains acetic acid, and the sour taste of lemons, limes and pineapples is caused by citric acid. Acids vary in strength; concentrated hydrochloric acid is much stronger than concentrated acetic acid, but citric acid, no matter how concentrated, is quite harmless.

Bases are also found in the home; washing and caustic soda are bases and ammonia, used in some household cleansers, is an alkali or soluble base. But the most commonly used base is limestone: it is widely used in agriculture, and is a vital ingredient in cement, plaster and concrete.

THE DIFFERENCE

An acid can be defined as a substance that generates ions of hydrogen (H^+): a base as one that generates hydroxyl ions (OH^-). Both of these actions occur in solution.

The medieval alchemist was aware that acids have the ability to dissolve metals; what he did not know is that the fizzing that takes place is caused by the creation of hydrogen. For example, when zinc dissolves in hydrochloric acid, the result is zinc chloride and hydrogen. Sulphuric acid reacts with iron to give ferrous sulphate and hydrogen. So an acid contains hydrogen and will dissolve a metal to form a salt.

What do alkalis do? If caustic potash (potassium hydroxide) is added to hydrochloric acid, we still get a salt, but no hydrogen is liberated. What has happened to the hydrogen in the acid? It has combined with the oxygen in the potassium hydroxide to form water. The definition of an alkali, therefore, could be a substance that reacts with an acid to form salt and water. Copper oxide reacts with sulphuric acid to produce copper sulphate (a salt) and water. But copper oxide is not an alkali – it is a harmless solid. Chemists therefore introduced

Acids and Bases

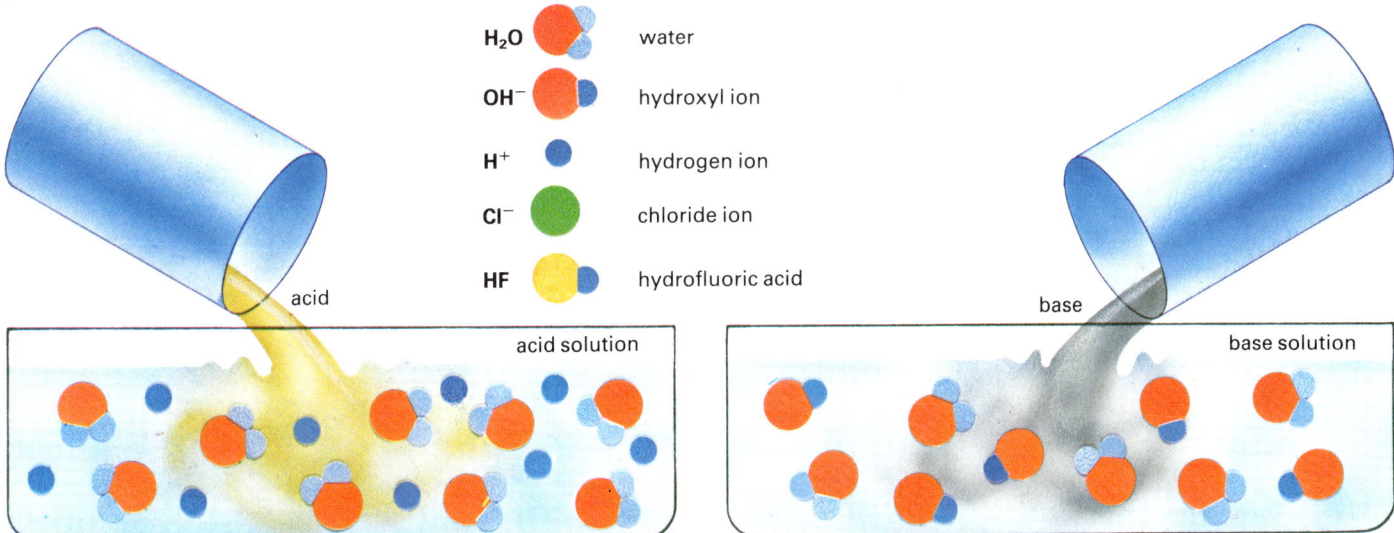

H_2O	water
OH^-	hydroxyl ion
H^+	hydrogen ion
Cl^-	chloride ion
HF	hydrofluoric acid

acid — acid solution

base — base solution

the word 'base' to define a compound that reacts with, or neutralises, an acid to form a salt and water, and a base that is soluble in water is called an alkali.

Early chemists combined the definitions of acids and bases to say that an acid is a substance with which a base reacts forming a salt and water, a definition which worked very well until more research was done.

When a compound is dissolved in water to form an acid, the hydrogen molecules are freed from the bond that holds them together and divide into their component atoms. As the hydrogen atoms only have one electron, they are hydrogen ions (H^+). When a base dissolves in water, individual atoms of oxygen bond with those of hydrogen to form hydroxyl ions (OH^-). This distinction gives us the means of measuring the strength of acids and bases.

This is measured in terms of the number of hydrogen ions produced in solution on a logarithmic pH (*potential of Hydrogen*) scale. Water is chemically neutral and has a pH value of 7; the concentration of H^+ and OH^- is equal (scientists write this as $H_2O \rightleftharpoons H^+ + OH^-$). Acid solutions have a pH value of less than 7 and base solutions of more than 7. The stronger the acid the lower the pH number, the more powerful the base, the higher the pH number (see the diagram on page 32). Because it is a logarithmic scale, a difference of one in the pH number indicates a difference of ten times in the strength of the substance. An acid of pH1 is ten times stronger than one of pH2, 100 times stronger than one of pH3, etc.

The strong acids are hydrochloric acid, nitric acid, hydrobromic acid and hydriodic acid. Strong bases include caustic soda (sodium hydroxide) and caustic potash (potassium hydroxide), both soluble in water and therefore alkalis.

Our bodies produce one of the strongest acids, the gastric juice – largely hydrochloric acid – which is used in the digestive system. And our very survival depends on the production of amino acids within the body.

Top: adding an acid or a base to a neutral solution creates an acid or a base solution. The former has an increased concentration of hydrogen ions, the latter hydroxyl ions, the strength of the acid or base being indicated by the amount of ions released. Above: a strong acid, such as hydrochloric, liberates more ions in solution than a weak one, such as hydrofluoric.

Weak acids and bases

The nearer to pH7 an acid or base is, the weaker it is; fewer hydrogen and hydroxyl ions are produced. Common weak acids include hydrogen citrate (citric acid) which occurs in the tangy fruits that we eat, hydrogen tartrate (cream of tartar) and, perhaps most common of all acids found in the house, ethanoic or acetic acid – vinegar. It is acid that causes milk to go sour; tiny organisms in the liquid produce lactic acid which causes the milk to curdle. An excess of acid in our stomachs may cause us pain. To remedy this we may take milk of magnesia – magnesium hydroxide, a weak base – which soon brings relief.

ACID + BASE = NEUTRALISATION

Why does the base, magnesium hydroxide, cancel out the pain caused by the excess acid? Because acids and bases neutralise each other, producing harmless salts and water. This is why tankers and storage containers for chemicals are often marked with instructions on what to use in the event of a leak. An acid leak will be neutralised by a base and vice versa.

USING ACIDS, BASES AND SALTS

All of these chemical substances have wide applications. Acids are used to etch metals, make explosives and fertilisers, in oil refining, paper manufacture and in the plastics and pharmaceutical industries. Alkalis and bases are used to make artificial fibres and soap. Salts are common to all living creatures and have industrial uses in the manufacture of medicines and pigments.

By combining acids and bases, industrial chemists are able to create compounds that are required in industry. Acids and alkalis are important to analytical chemists in identifying and testing the purity of minerals. Gold is tested by the application of acid, pure gold remaining unmarked by it. Poorer quality gold stains and corrodes as the acid reacts with the impurities. The quality is determined by increasing the strength of the acid at each testing.

pH VALUES OF SOME COMMON SUBSTANCES

Substance	pH value
Gastric juice	1·4
Lemon juice	2·1
Orange juice	2·8
Wine	3·5
Tomato juice	4·1
Expresso coffee	5·0
Urine	6·0
Milk	6·9
Distilled water	7·0
Blood	7·4
Bicarbonate of soda	8·5
Household ammonia	11·9

Above: most substances except distilled water (ordinary water with all the impurities removed) are either acid or base; the pH values of a number of common ones and solids are shown here. Below left: salts produced by the reaction of bases and acids have many uses. Here we see how a number of sodium salts are used in our day-to-day lives. Below right: the pH scale. Acids give solutions with pH values from 1–7, and bases from 7–14. Water, or a solution with a pH value of 7, is neutral. Bottom: various indicators and how they react to solutions of differing pH values are shown in this table. The use of these indicators is not just the concern of chemists but has tremendous application in industry and agriculture.

ACID OR BASE?

One of the problems faced by analytical chemists is how to tell whether a solution is acid or base. To do so they use substances called indicators – compounds that readily change colour depending on the pH of the solution in which it is dissolved.

Several indicators are found in the kitchen: for example, the juice in which red cabbage has been boiled turns red when an acid is added (such as vinegar or orange juice) but bluish-green when a base such as washing soda is added. The most well-known indicator used in laboratories is litmus, which is made from lichens. A strip of litmus paper will turn bright red when it is dipped into an acid and bright blue when dipped in a base. Another one, Congo Red, has the opposite effect; it turns blue in an acid and red in an alkali.

Indicators can also be used to test the strength of an acid or base, and papers are available which are dyed with a range of indicators. These have characteristic colours at a given pH so that the scientist can tell if the solution he is testing is pH3 or pH4, and so on.

The use of indicators is also important when salts are being made by mixing acids and bases together, when it is vital that the exact amount of acid and base have been added to neutralise each other. The chemist will add the acid to the base very gradually, testing all the time with an indicator. When it begins to change colour, he knows that neutrality has almost been achieved.

Analytical chemists use indicators to test the strength of an acid or base. To find the strength of an alkali, for instance, he will add it to an acid of known strength. When neutrality has been achieved, the strength of the acid can be used to calculate the strength of the alkali.

ACIDS AND SOILS

It is important for farmers to know the exact acid content of the soil on their land as it has a considerable effect on the growth of plants. Over-acid soil can be counteracted or neutralised by the use of calcium hydroxide (lime) or calcium carbonate (chalk).

Different crops need different levels of acidity; potatoes, for instance, grow well in an acid soil, but wheat prefers an alkaline soil. Most soils in Britain have pH values of between 4 and 9, but soils tend to become more acidic as the years pass if they are not treated. The reasons for this is that carbon dioxide and other acidic gases dissolve in the rain as it falls, and rainwater washes away the basic substances in the soil. The acid in the rain leaches the soil, dissolving calcium carbonate; and acid soils prevent the decomposition of humus – dead plant material – resulting in waterlogged soil. Agricultural technologists can test the acidity of a soil and advise the farmers on how best to treat it.

SOME SODIUM SALTS AND THEIR USES

Salt	Chemical formula	Use
Sodium bicarbonate	$2NaHCO_3$	digestive
Sodium chlorate	$NaClO_3$	herbicide
Sodium hypochlorite	$NaOCl$	disinfectant
Sodium nitrate	$NaNO_3$	fertiliser
Sodium sulphate	Na_2SO_4	liver salts
Sodium sulphide	NA_2S	detergent
Sodium thiosulphate	$Na_2S_2O_3$	photographic fixative

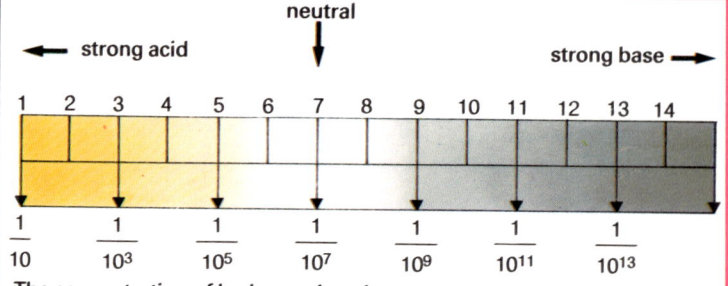

The concentration of hydrogen ions increases towards strong acid; the concentration of hydroxyl ions increases towards strong base.

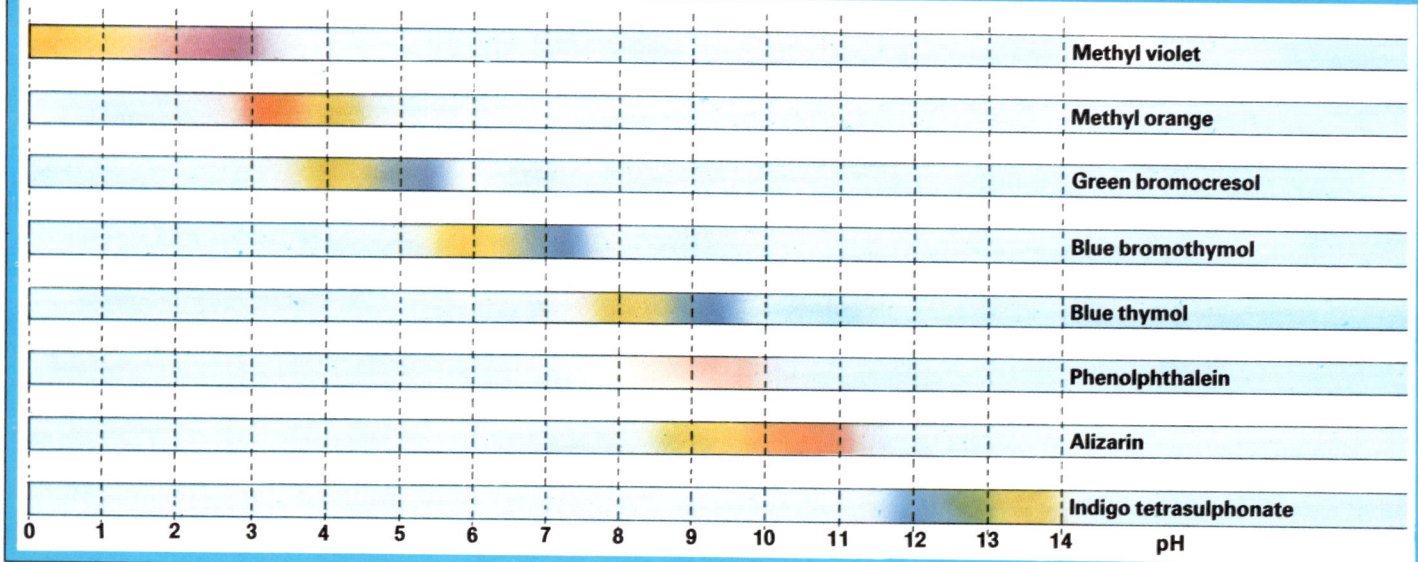

Methyl violet

Methyl orange

Green bromocresol

Blue bromothymol

Blue thymol

Phenolphthalein

Alizarin

Indigo tetrasulphonate

The Golden Gate Bridge in San Francisco is one of the most beautiful structures in the world. Sweeping over the bay, it carries enormous amounts of traffic every day. The towers supporting the suspension cables and the girders of the roadway are made of high-quality steel; the material which, perhaps, most of all represents the whole story of man's technological advancement. Strong and resilient, yet flexible enough to cope with the movements of traction and torsion, steel has become the main component not only of the great constructions of the last two centuries and in vehicles of all types, but also of simple everyday domestic objects such as cutlery, taps and sinks, and even jewellery. The processing of iron ores to produce various grades of steel is one of the most important heavy industries of the twentieth century, so much so that it plays a fundamental part in the industrial development of a country. The iron and steel industry is, in fact, the base of the mechanical and metallurgical industries and the backbone of the economic structure of an industrial nation. From its small beginnings in the Middle Ages, the steel industry has grown into one of the most important in the world, producing well in excess of one million tonnes every day.

Iron and Steel

STEEL MAKING

Steel does not occur naturally in the Earth. It is a mixture of iron and carbon, and can be alloyed with other metals to give steels of varying qualities, according to their composition.

Fortunately for us (for we now rely on steel for a vast number of purposes) iron is the second most abundant metal in the world; 6% of all metals, only 2% less than aluminium. But it does not occur naturally in its pure state and has to be extracted from ore-bearing materials such as limonite, pyrite, hematite and magnetite, all of which are oxides or sulphides of iron.

The iron that is extracted by smelting (called pig iron) contains up to 4% carbon which makes it hard but brittle. If the carbon content is reduced to less than 1·7% the alloy is called steel; if it is between 2 and 3·5% it is cast iron (which also contains small amounts of silicon, sulphur, manganese and phosphorus).

The diagram above illustrates the principal processing plant involved in the manufacture of iron and steel.

1. The iron-bearing ores and limestone flux (which is used to remove impurities from the ores) are assembled ready to be used.

2. Coke is produced from coal in special coke ovens. Coke is 80% carbon.

3. The charge (raw material) is fed into a blast furnace where it is reduced to molten iron with a slag floating on top. The slag is run off through a 'slag notch' into moulds. It is used for road making and paving materials, building blocks, and in the manufacture of cement. It is also processed into slag wool, for insulation. The iron is either used in its molten state or cast into 'pigs'. Some of it is sent directly to the iron foundries where it is used in the manufacture of cast iron products.

4. Most of the pig iron is sent to the steel works where it is heated with scrap steel and the carbon content reduced by oxidation to less than 1·7%. Other metals can be added to give steel of the desired quality.

5. The steel is then sent to foundries and mills where it is forged, rolled or cast into a wide range of goods.

The steel that is produced is resilient and flexible, and it is stronger and more easily worked than iron. Various types of steel can be made, such as mild steels for engineering and structural work, carbon steels for components and tools, alloy steels for their special properties (stainless steel is one of these; it is made by mixing steel and nickel to give a tough metal that is resistant to rust and corrosion) and high-speed steels containing tungsten and chromium, which are used in the machine-tool industry.

Right: Iron and steel works are usually situated close to a port so that the raw materials can be brought in conveniently.

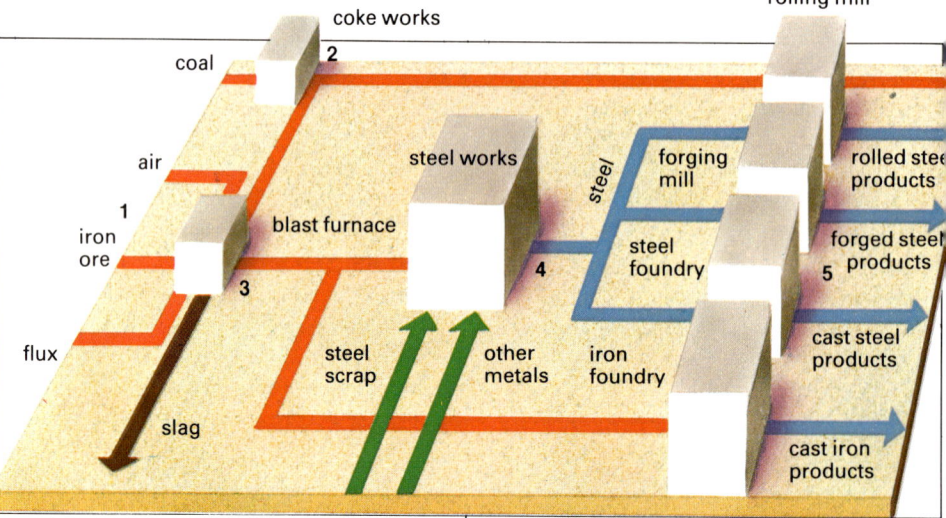

The blast furnace

The furnace in which the iron ore is converted into pig iron is a steel-encased structure closed at the top by a double-lock system to prevent gases escaping.

The furnace is charged with coke, ore and flux through the lock at the top. Pressurised air heated to 500–900° C (932–1,652° F) is piped in through ten or twelve nozzles called tuyères, which causes partial combustion of the coke at the bottom forming carbon monoxide. Just above the blast inlet, the temperature reaches 1,600° C (2,912° F) or more. The gas rises and, reacting with the iron ore, reduces it to iron which sinks through the coke, melting as it becomes hotter and absorbing carbon from the carbon monoxide. The waste gases are collected, cleaned, and used to preheat the air for the furnace. The molten pig iron, at a temperature of up to 1,450° C (2,642° F), collects at the hearth bottom and is tapped off every 3–6 hours. The slag passes down with the iron and floats on top of the molten metal when it reaches the bottom. It, also, is tapped off regularly.

Basic oxygen steelmaking

Today, most pig iron is processed into steel by the basic oxygen process. Up to 350 tonnes of molten pig iron together with some steel scrap is put into the furnace, a pear-shaped vessel. A water-cooled tube or lance is lowered into it, which blows a jet of pure oxygen on to the surface of metal, and lime is added to form a slag. The oxygen combines with the excess carbon and burns it away and the other impurities are oxidised and pass into the slag. The steel is ready after about forty minutes; the slag is poured off first, and the steel then transferred for casting into ingots.

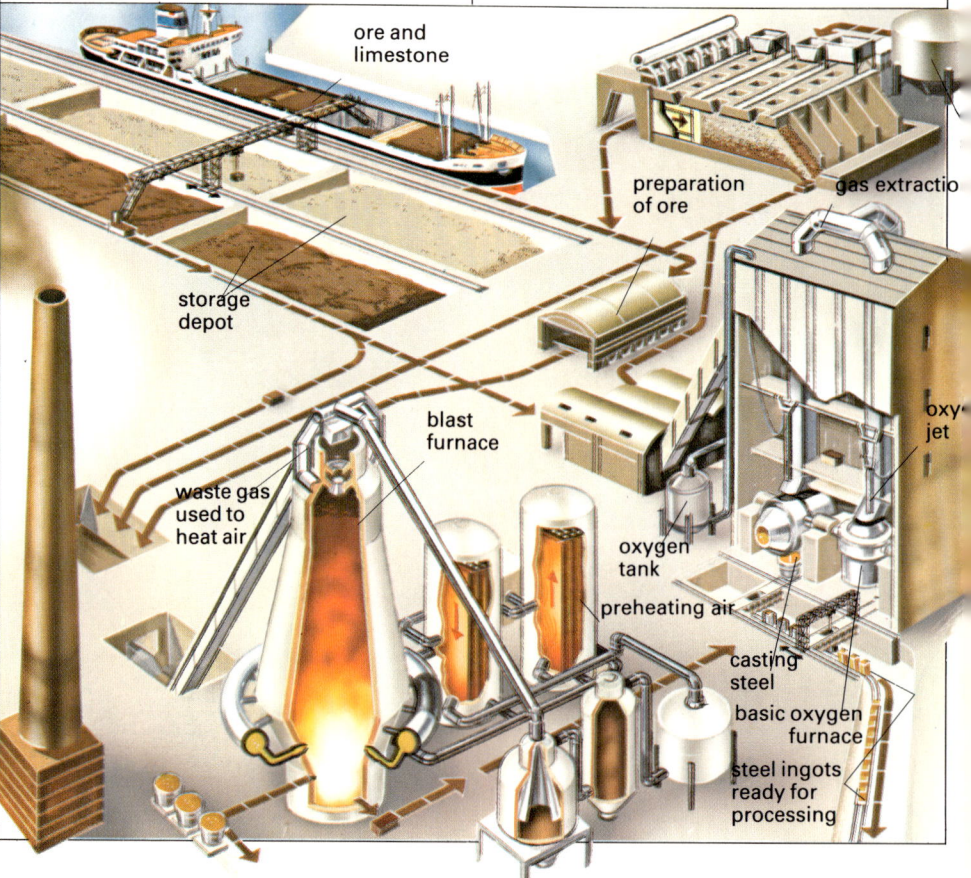

PROCESSING STEEL

When the steel comes from the furnace it is usually poured into moulds and cools into ingots. Moulding molten steel is known as casting. In continuous casting the molten metal is poured from the ladle into a basin from where it flows through a nozzle into an open-ended, vertical, water-cooled mould from which it emerges semi-solid. The casting is further cooled by cold water jets and controlled by rollers. The cool, solid metal is cut into strips of the required length.

The main methods of working with hot metal are shown above right. These are forging, rolling and section rolling. Forging, the oldest method, is shaping hot metal by means of repeated hammer blows or progressive squeezing. In drop forging a mechanical hammer forces the metal into the die cavity (1a, 1b and 1c above). In rolling (2) the hot metal is squeezed between powerful rollers which produces flat steel shapes, such as plates or strips, of the desired thickness. Steel processed in this way is used in shipbuilding, car manufacturing and similar industries. In section rolling (3) the steel is shaped as it is rolled into square, round or oval sections or to produce girders, rails, joists etc, used in the construction industry. The pressure rollers can be adjusted to give the required dimensions. There are also a number of cold working processes which increase the hardness and strength of the metal.

White hot molten steel runs from the tilted ladle, down a channel into ingot moulds. Scenes such as this are no longer as common in Britain as they once were; world recession and a slump in the demand for steel has caused many steel works to be closed down.

Kilometre after kilometre of pipelines, storage tanks, condensing and distilling towers: the whole area looking, perhaps, like the futuristic imaginings of an early science-fiction writer. It is in fact, a panorama typical of the chemical industry, the modern chemical complex. Today's chemical industry is as important as the iron industries were in the last quarter of the nineteenth century and the first part of the twentieth. The huge investment required to develop the industry is well worth it when we consider that the products and by-products touch every part of our lives. We depend on the chemical industry to supply foods, fertilisers, drugs and fibres. It has become, in a relatively short time, one of the most important of industries.

The Chemical Industry

ALL AROUND US

The modern chemical industry did not suddenly appear overnight. About two hundred years of painstaking research and experiment went into laying the foundation-stones on which the modern industry is built.

Dedicated scientists have had to study the elements and the ways in which they combine with each other to form compounds, and how these compounds could be used. Some scientists have spent their entire careers in the study of just one particular area of specialisation, more often than not for little reward.

Gradually the pieces were fitted together and the chemical industry came into being. At first it was small, employing only a few people, but today it is a multi-million dollar industry employing hundreds of thousands of men and women around the world and producing a wide range of products that we now take for granted.

The cornerstone of the industry is the industrial chemist, who initiates research programmes to produce a chemical or chemical reaction that will fill a material need and, if it can be made economically worth while, will become the basis of a commercial enterprise.

When we realise the importance of the industry, it will come as little surprise to learn that Britain's largest public company with a turnover as large as the national incomes of many small countries is ICI – Imperial Chemical Industries.

Catalyst	Function
Iron oxide	Speeds up the hydrogen/nitrogen reaction to form ammonia
Vanadium pentoxide	Used in the manufacture of sulphuric acid
Oxides and silicates of aluminium, aluminium and magnesium	Used in the petro-chemical industry for catalytic cracking of molecules

THE USE OF CATALYSTS

Many chemical reactions can be speeded up by the use of catalysts, substances that alter the rate at which the reactions take place without themselves changing.

In the commercial production of ammonia, used as a refrigerant and in the manufacture of fertilisers and explosives, an iron oxide catalyst, with traces of aluminium oxide and potassium oxide to encourage the bonding of nitrogen and hydrogen to form ammonia (NH_3), is used. Heaters are used to start the reaction, but once it has begun the heat it produces maintains a temperature of 500° C (932° F). The gases are pumped over the catalyst in the converter at high pressure, being heated on the way by the hot gases leaving it. Some of the nitrogen and hydrogen combines, forming ammonia which is removed and cooled, and the remaining gases are recirculated. Overheating is prevented by the circulation of cooling gas around the converter and through pipes in the catalyst.

THE FATHER OF THE INDUSTRY

In 1775 the Paris Academy of Sciences, concerned that the high price of soap put it out of reach of many Parisians and was thus indirectly responsible for the spread of some diseases, offered a prize (at today's prices, of £5,000) to anyone who could devise a cheap way of producing sodium carbonate – used in the manufacture of soap, glass and paper.

It took Nicholas Leblanc, a French doctor, fourteen years to perfect a process using chalk, salt, charcoal and sulphuric acid. But the Academy refused to give him the prize, as they thought the process uneconomic.

Leblanc managed to raise financial backing and set up a sodium carbonate plant in the St. Denis suburb of Paris. The process involved heating salt in sulphuric acid to produce sodium sulphate which was then heated with carbon and chalk to form a mixture of sodium carbonate and calcium sulphide. Water was added and, as only the sodium carbonate (soda) dissolved, it could be separated and evaporated to yield crystals of the desired chemical.

Leblanc's factory covered two acres and was laid out in such a way that the handling of the chemicals was kept to a minimum. It was the first real chemical factory and the first of any kind to operate on the modern system of a constant flow of ingredients.

Leblanc's process made soap manufacture much cheaper and brought down the price of glass and paper, just as the Academy had hoped. Leblanc is rightly regarded as the father of industrial chemistry.

Left: a soap factory in 1770, before Leblanc's cheap, mass-produced chemical was available. Within a few years soap manufacture had passed from being a skilled job to mass-production.

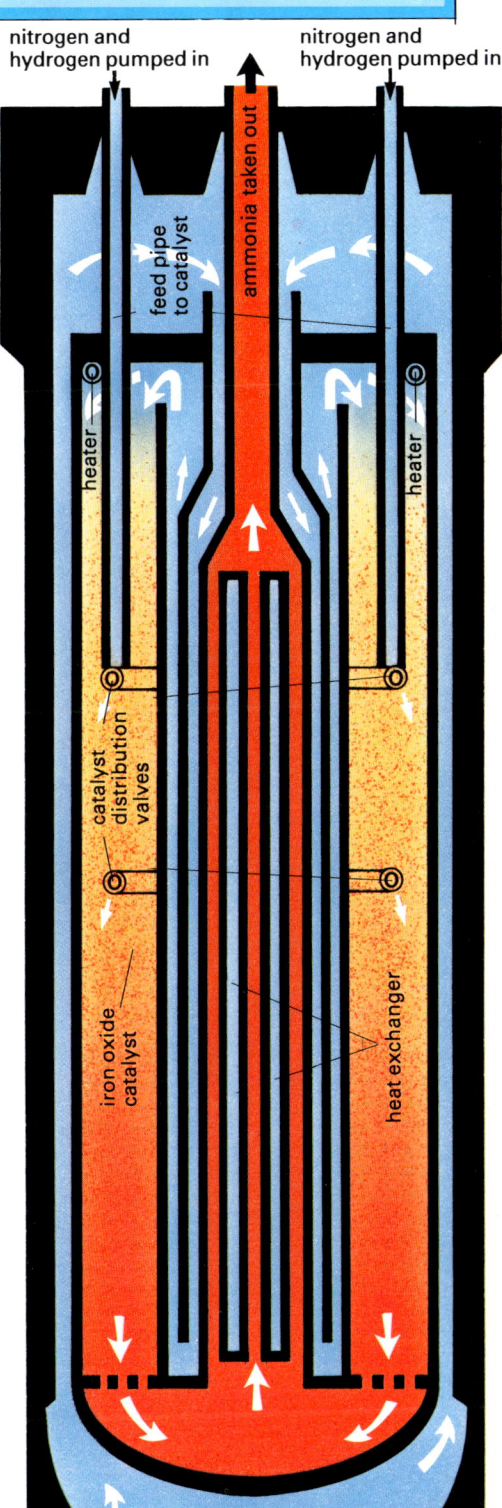

nitrogen and hydrogen pumped in

nitrogen and hydrogen pumped in

ammonia taken out

feed pipe to catalyst

heater

heater

catalyst distribution valves

iron oxide catalyst

heat exchanger

coolant

PRODUCING PHOSPHORUS

Phosphorus is widely used in the manufacture of many items, for example detergents, fertilisers and in the food, pharmaceutical and metallurgical industries. It only occurs in nature as a compound, the main source being calcium phosphate – $Ca_3(PO_4)_2$ – which is found in minerals such as rock phosphate. The phosphorus is produced by heating calcium phosphate with carbon (coke) and silicon dioxide (silica) – SiO_2. The phosphate rock is fed, with coke and silica chippings, into an electric furnace, an airtight steel tank with a tap hole for slag. Ferrophosphorus, an alloy, can also be tapped off. At 1,500° C, the phosphate reacts with the silica, forming phosphorus pentoxide – P_2O_5 – and a calcium silicate slag – $CaSiO_3$. The phosphorus pentoxide is reduced by the coke and forms phosphorus vapour and carbon monoxide. The slag is run off and used in road-making, and the gaseous

phosphate storage silo

silica storage silo

coke storage silo

phosphate

carbon electrodes

coke feed conveyor belt

feeder

pump

storage tank

storage tank

pump

mixture of phosphorus vapour and dust, and carbon monoxide, is discharged and passed through an electrostatic dust precipitator. The dust is filtered out and recovered, as the phosphorus in it can be used. The cleaned gas passes into a condenser where it is washed with warm water to lower the temperature and allow the phosphorus to condense and separate

from the carbon monoxide, which is removed and burnt off. At this stage the phosphorus enters a closed system where sodium carbonate – Na_2CO_3 – and water are added to neutralise any phosphoric acid which may have formed and the residual

gas is eliminated. The phosphorus goes into a storage container where the remaining vapour is drawn off and recirculated through the condensing system. The pure phosphorus is pumped to airtight storage tanks before being delivered to customers.

silica

coke

electrode

electrostatic dust precipitator

phosphorus vapour and dust + carbon monoxide

cleaned gas

heating bars

burning off carbon monoxide

water for condensation

reusable dust removed

phosphorus container

molten phosphorus

CO

CO

suction valve

molten slag

electric furnace

H_2O

Na_2CO_3

phosphorus + CO + H_2O

neutraliser

phosphorus

separator

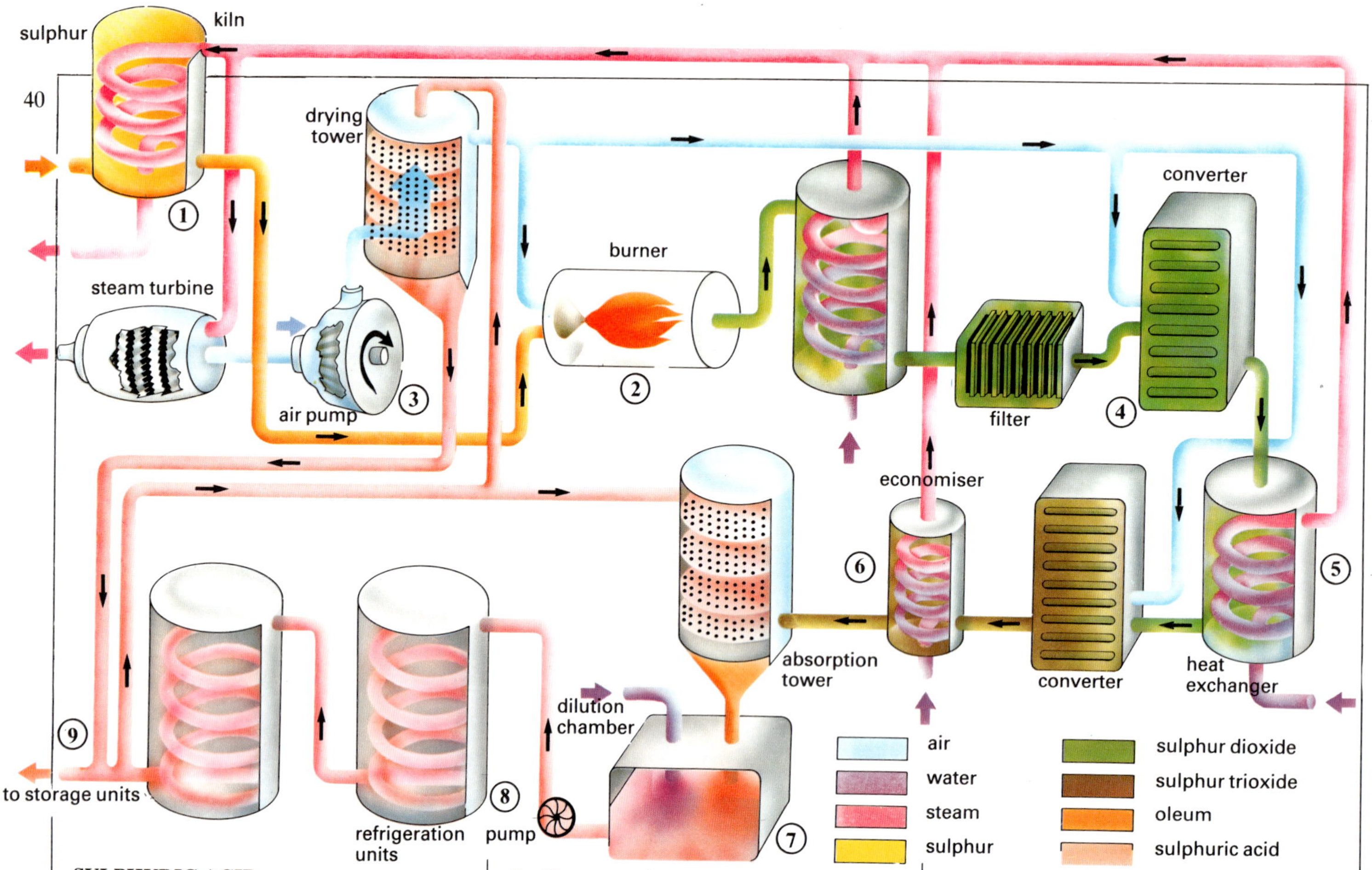

Diagram labels (top):

sulphur kiln

drying tower

steam turbine

air pump ③

② burner

converter

filter ④

economiser

absorption tower

heat exchanger

converter ⑤

⑥

dilution chamber

refrigeration units

pump ⑧

⑨

to storage units

⑦

Legend:

- air
- water
- steam
- sulphur
- sulphur dioxide
- sulphur trioxide
- oleum
- sulphuric acid

SULPHURIC ACID

One of the most important of all industrial acids is sulphuric acid (H_2SO_4). It has many uses, for example in the manufacture of fertilisers, detergents, explosives, paints, fibres, and in the oil-refining processes.

Sulphuric acid is produced in one of two ways from sulphur dioxide. In the lead chamber process the acid produced is not of a very high state of purity but still has many uses. The contact process, shown in the diagram above, produces acid of a high degree of purity.

In the contact process, sulphur is first vaporised in a kiln heated with steam (1), and the resulting vapour is burnt in air (2) which has been dried by passing it through sulphuric acid (a good drying agent). When combined with oxygen, the vapour becomes sulphur dioxide (SO_2). The heat produced is used to drive a steam turbine and an air pump (3). The sulphur dioxide is cleaned with filters to remove dust and impurities, mixed with pure, dry air, and oxidised in a converter (4) at a temperature of 450°C, using vanadium pentoxide as a catalyst. This produces sulphur trioxide (SO_3) which passes through a heat exchanger (5) and into a second converter which helps to purify the sulphur trioxide. The heat from this process is also recovered (6) and reused in the system. As sulphur trioxide does not dissolve easily in water it is absorbed into sulphuric acid, producing fuming sulphuric acid or oleum, to which a regulated stream of water is added (7) producing highly concentrated sulphuric acid. The acid is then cooled (8) and pumped to storage areas (9).

Fertiliser manufacture: ammonia (1) is made into nitric acid (2), then used to neutralise this to make ammonium nitrate (3). Potassium chloride (4) is added. Sulphuric acid (6) from sulphur (5) is added to calcium phosphate (7) dissolved in phosphoric acid (8) which, with ammonia, gives ammonium nitrate (9). Calcium phosphate is also treated with sulphuric acid to produce 'superphosphates'. The chemicals are then mixed into a base (10), granulated (11) and dried (12).

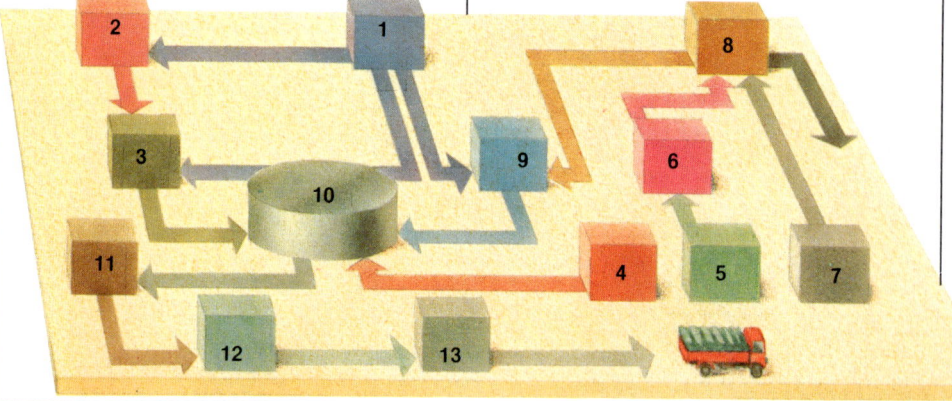

MAKING IT WORTHWHILE

The base materials used by the chemical industry often occur naturally and abundantly, for example substances such as oxygen, nitrogen, hydrogen, sulphur and chlorine (contained in rock salt). Also the chemical reactions on which the processes of industrial production are based are often very simple. The difficulty lies in financing the research and development and changing the laboratory experiments into processes which are economic and sufficiently adequate to meet the demands of the market.

Although the reactions and their chemical symbols may appear simple, the same reactions would not have taken place if one of the reacting substances or one of the numerous factors involved – temperature, pressure, catalytic action etc – had been different. The laboratory experiment must be set up on a large scale, and if this pilot plant can be run successfully, it can then be turned into a manufacturing industry.

The cost of setting up a chemical plant is enormous. Hence the chemical industry is controlled by giant corporations with funds, rather than the chemists themselves, and the commercial future of the laboratory work is in the hands of businessmen and accountants who must investigate the profitability of using the scientist's information and applying it commercially.

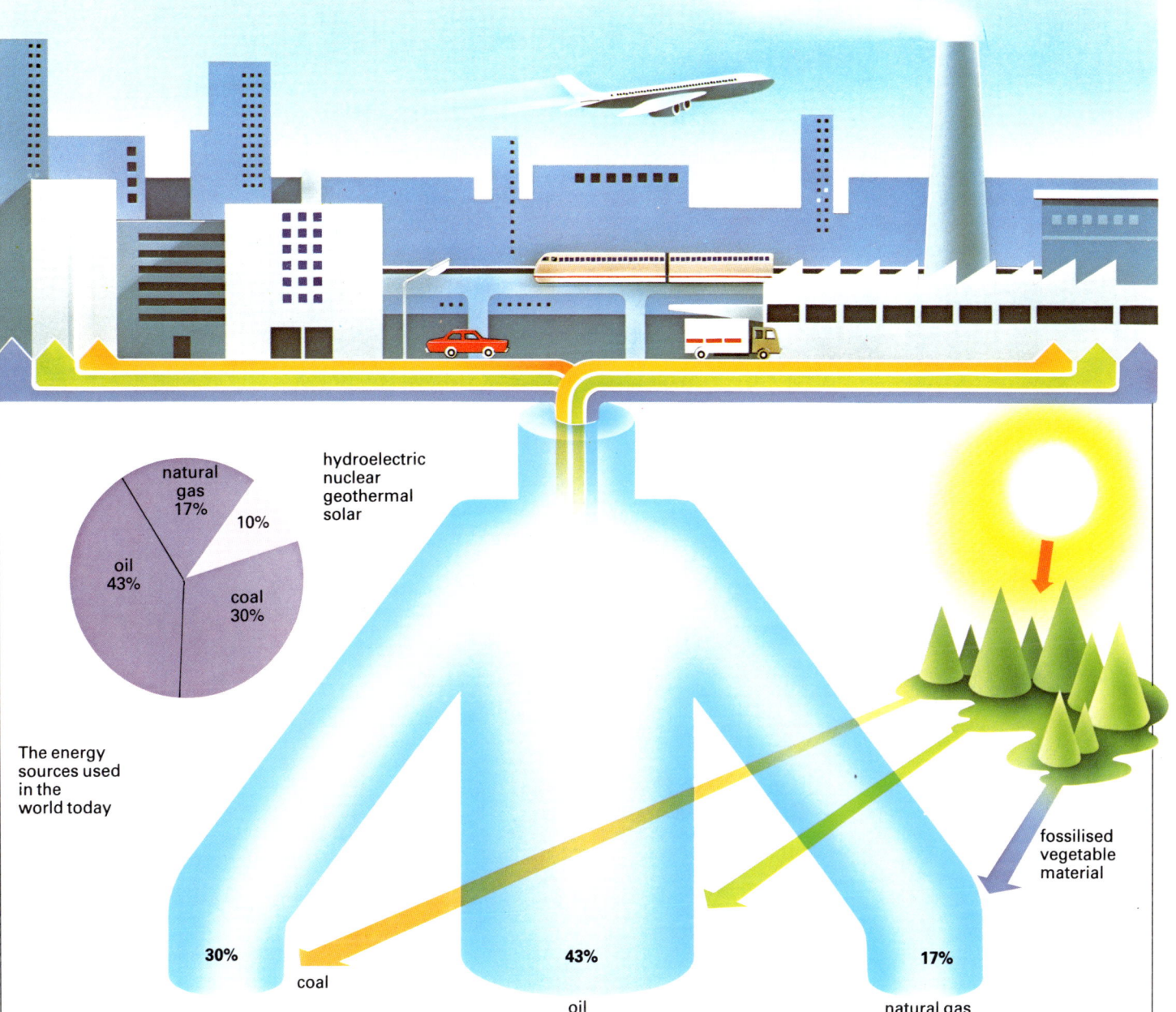

natural gas 17%

10%

oil 43%

coal 30%

hydroelectric
nuclear
geothermal
solar

The energy sources used in the world today

fossilised vegetable material

30% coal

43% oil

17% natural gas

Chemical Energy

Twentieth-century society is dependent on the production and consumption of energy to fuel its industries, transport its food and manufactured items, light and heat its homes, power its tractors and combine harvesters and to keep its ships, trains, planes and road vehicles on the move. Ninety per cent of the energy that we use comes to us from fossil fuels – storehouses of the sun's colossal power. When we burn coal, oil or natural gas we release the chemical energy packed within, and there is hardly any aspect of our lives that is not ultimately dependent on the use of this energy in some form or other.

ENERGY AND CHEMICAL CHANGES

Although scientists are constantly researching new energy sources we still depend on the energy that is released during chemical changes for most of our power.

When chemical bonds are broken or changed, and heat (energy) is given out, the reaction is called exothermic; one of the most important examples of this is the combustion of a fuel. Petrol vapour in a car engine is ignited by a spark and combustion occurs in a confined space, producing the power to drive the engine. The bonds between the hydrocarbons (carbon atoms bonded together and to hydrogen atoms) are broken and new ones are formed with oxygen, the reaction giving out more energy than that supplied by the spark that activated it – an exothermic reaction. Most common chemical reactions are exothermic, but not all reactions liberate energy;

some need to take in energy if they are to occur. These are called endothermic reactions.

The man who first realised that heat is a form of energy was Benjamin Thompson, better known as Count Rumford, who put forward a theory that heat was a form of motion, not, as had previously been accepted, a fluid called 'caloric' which penetrated between the tiniest particles of a body. Thompson was astonished by the large amounts of heat generated by the internal boring of cannons, and carried out systematic experiments to measure it. This led him to believe that heat was produced by friction; it resulted from the conversion of mechanical energy.

With heat being the product of so many chemical reactions, we have at our disposal a ready means of producing power from chemical changes.

USING CHEMICAL ENERGY

When a chemical reaction liberates energy, the resultants (products) of the reaction will have less energy than the original reactants. They are said to be more stable.

Methane is a high energy gas composed of four atoms of hydrogen and one of carbon (CH_4). When it reacts with two diatomic molecules of oxygen (O_2), the carbon combines with two of the oxygen atoms to form carbon dioxide (CO_2) and the four hydrogen atoms combine with the other two oxygen atoms to produce two molecules of water (H_2O). During this process heat is given off, which can be measured in calories. A calorie is defined as the quantity of heat that raises one gram of water (usually at 15° C) by one degree centigrade, but it has now, in scientific work, been superseded by the joule, equal to 4·184 calories, which is a unit of energy rather than heat.

We use methane every day in our kitchens. It is the natural gas found in huge deposits under the North Sea. Before these reserves were found, natural gas from Algeria was shipped to Britain as a liquid – cooled to −106° C (−159° F) – then reconverted and pumped into the gas grid.

The chemical cell

A chemical cell will convert a chemical change directly into electricity without going through the intermediate heat stage. One of the simplest has a zinc rod acting as an anode (positive electrode) in dilute sulphuric acid, which becomes zinc sulphate solution, in a porous pot of unglazed porcelain. This is in a copper sulphate solution containing a copper rod which acts as a cathode (negative electrode). The porous pot allows the ions to move from one solution to the other, and the chemical change that occurs results in a flow of electricity.

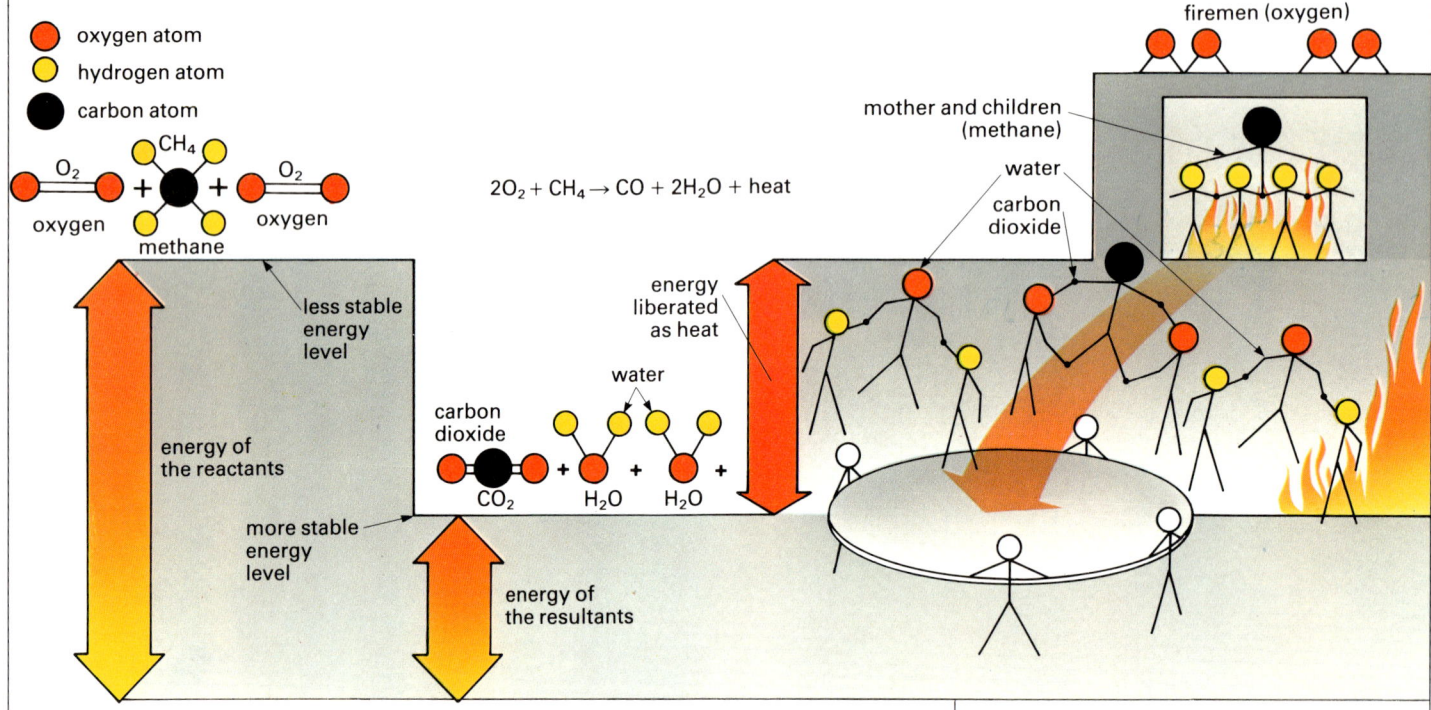

$$2O_2 + CH_4 \rightarrow CO + 2H_2O + heat$$

The chemical reaction that occurs when methane is combined with oxygen can be likened to what is happening in the diagram above (right). A mother (the carbon atom of methane) and her four children (the hydrogen atoms) are trapped in a burning building – an unstable situation. Four firemen appear two by two (two diatomic molecules of oxygen) on the roof to rescue them. Two of the firemen carry the mother (forming carbon dioxide – CO_2) and the others carry two children each (forming two molecules of water – H_2O) and they all jump down to the safety – stability – of the canvas below. The kinetic energy of their fall can be compared to the energy released as heat by the reaction, the result of the redistribution of chemical bonds.

OXIDATION

Oxygen is a highly reactive element, willing to combine readily with other elements and compounds to form various oxides.

Sometimes the results of oxidation are quite spectacular, such as when we strike a match. The heat caused by the friction that results when we rub the match head along the rough edge of the box encourages the phosphorus to combine with the oxygen in the potassium chlorate contained in the head, which also contains sulphur and manganese oxide. The result is a small explosion – the chemicals burst into flames, causing the wood to catch fire.

Other examples are much less spectacular and take place over a period of time. Rust is the result of iron combining with oxygen to form iron oxide. Moisture encourages the reaction to take place.

There are cases where oxidation could be dangerous and steps are taken to prevent it. In a tungsten light bulb, for instance, the electric current heats the metal to very high temperatures at which point, under normal circumstances, an explosive oxidation reaction would occur. This is avoided by pumping all the air out of the glass envelope that surrounds the wire filament.

The term oxidation is now used to describe any reaction in which an element combines with another and loses electrons.

Oxidation, which causes a match to burn and paper to turn yellow, must be prevented to stop a light bulb from exploding.

Explosive energy

Some materials give off energy when they explode on heating, as a result of friction, being struck or being ignited, with violent reactions. Some materials will react violently when exposed to light. Explosives differ in the amount of gas that they produce per kilogram of explosive, the amount of heat liberated, the detonation velocity, the pressure that the hot gases exert upon their immediate surroundings and in the immense power developed.

Explosives consist of either mixtures of substances which react with each other, or chemical compounds that release energy on decomposition. Once ignition or decomposition has been started reactions are initiated at adjacent points, setting off chain reactions which spread through the explosive in a fraction of a second.

The energy that results from explosion has obvious military uses as well as being useful in mining and quarrying. To be efficient, explosives should only explode when required to do so. Hence the use of primers or detonators which initiate an explosion with a small quantity of highly sensitive material – which explodes easily on being lit, struck or subjected to friction, or by using electricity to create a spark which ignites the explosive. In the early days of cannon warfare, a lighted taper was used to ignite the powder which, if it was not properly packed, could explode prematurely, causing as much injury to the firer as to the enemy.

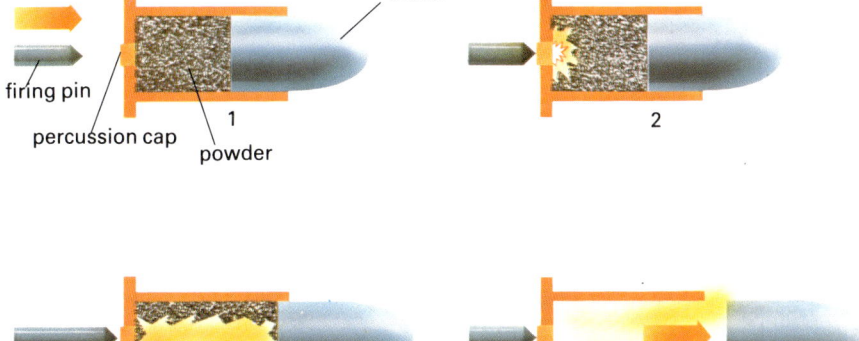

Below: light can also supply the energy to start a chemical reaction, acting as a 'detonator'. The reaction of hydrogen and chlorine gas in the dark is normally slow unless they are heated, but becomes explosive in sunlight. In (1) the molecules of hydrogen and chlorine remain separate. However, when exposed to strong light (2) they react violently (3) – the bonds holding the molecules together are broken and the hydrogen combines with the chlorine (4) to form hydrogen chloride (HCl). The study of chemical reactions caused by light, or producing light, is called photochemistry.

Top: the spectacular bursts of sparks and coloured lights of a firework display. Fireworks are small explosive devices with various chemicals added to the gunpowder, which is a mixture of sulphur, charcoal and saltpetre (potassium nitrate), to create the special effects.

Above: the firing pin of a gun striking the percussion cap causes the initiatory composition inside to detonate, which in turn ignites the nitrocellulose powder in the case. This burns with such power in a confined space that it causes the bullet to be ejected with great force.

- hydrogen molecule
- chlorine molecule
- hydrogen atom
- chlorine atom
- hydrogen chloride molecules

Science and Technology at Work

In a cloud of steam and with a great deal of huffing and puffing, this revolutionary vehicle moves towards a brick wall, the men on and around it quite powerless to stop it . . . The work of scientists who developed the power of steam had been applied by technologists to produce a new method of transport – one that crashed on its first outing! But science was no longer something to be studied by a few; it was becoming one of man's most important allies.

Nicholas-Joseph Cugnot, a French artillery officer, started to build in 1769 what many experts consider to be the true ancestor of the motor-car. Powered by steam, it did work, but its maiden trip was something of a disaster as can be seen here. A partial reconstruction of Cugnot's 'car' can still be seen in Paris.

TECHNOLOGICAL PROGRESS

When man invented the simple wooden plough pulled by oxen, he increased the potential of the land; he could grow crops over a much wider area than could previously be cultivated. Although he was unaware of it, he was actually beginning to apply scientific thinking to agriculture.

The introduction of the metal ploughshare was another important step. Such an implement could dig deeper furrows into harder ground and was much more efficient than the simple wooden plough, especially with the later addition of the mould board which turned the ploughed earth at the side of the furrow.

The invention of the internal combustion engine, the increase in our knowledge of metals, the invention of the rubber tyre and technological and scientific advances in other areas have resulted in today's multiple ploughs linked to a tractor, enabling one operator to cover in a few hours an area of land that his ancestors would have thought impossible to cultivate.

The wooden plough *at first was probably little more than a branch of wood, used to break up the soil, without any changes being made to it. But eventually, Man began to adapt the basic shape and add handles to make the plough more effective, although still, by our way of thinking, very primitive.*

The metal ploughshare *which is still used in some parts of the world. Pulled by horses and other draught animals, it required some considerable scientific and technological advances to be made before it became effective. Eventually steam power was developed to pull a plough across a field, but horse-drawn ploughs were not superseded until the invention of the tractor.*

The tractor-drawn plough *which is used in all developed agricultural countries, is a triumph of technology. It is quick and economic, and enables one farmhand to do the work that would previously have needed many men, and to do it more efficiently.*

MAKING LIFE BETTER FOR US

Science and technology, working hand in hand, have made the quality of life in the twentieth century what it is today. Life is almost unimaginable without the motor-car and aeroplane to carry us quickly from place to place; without television and radio to entertain us; without the artificial fibres that go into so many of the clothes that we wear today, as well as into the furnishings of our houses and offices.

It is difficult to think how we would get along without electricity and gas to provide the power that we use, and today nuclear energy is a reality. Civilisation would possibly not be so advanced if we had been unable to refine crude oil into the petrol and other chemicals that we now depend on.

Medical researchers have given us new drugs and introduced new treatments that have resulted in longer and healthier lives for millions of people in the developed countries.

Agriculturalists have bred new varieties of plants suitable for cultivation in places where the original strains could not be grown, making it possible for new areas of land to come under cultivation, and to ease the world's food shortage.

It is the scientists who come up with new

Physicists with a deep knowledge of the laws of mechanics and electricity have made possible the machinery used.

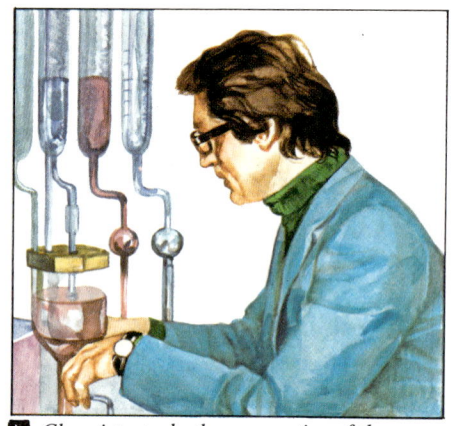

Chemists study the properties of the materials used in the process and how they react with each other.

Botanists develop new strains of plants, encouraging the properties that they require to make them more suitable for use.

Engineers use aspects of many sciences when designing the machinery and deciding how it is most efficiently used.

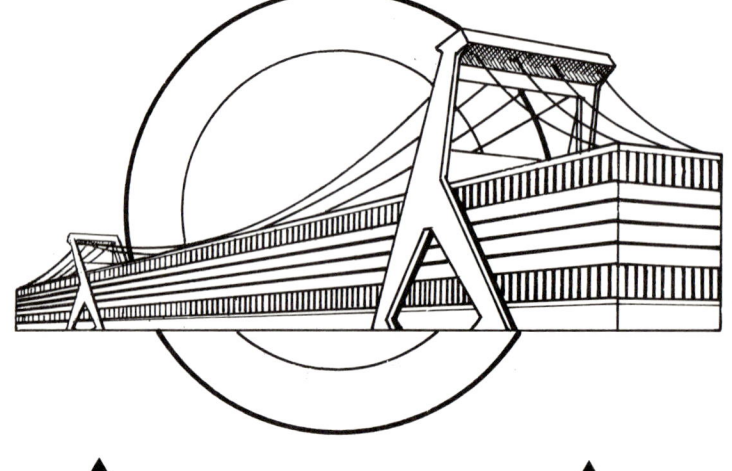

Factory hands, many of them very skilled, control the machines used on the factory floor in the various stages of production.

Technicians ensure that the machinery is in good working order and arrange for regular repairs and services.

In the laboratories, researchers study new theories and experiment with new materials to assess their efficiency.

propositions and the technicians and engineers who put these into effect that we must thank for much of what we take for granted today.

The work of many of these specialists is vital in industry. In the illustration below we can see science and technology in action in the production of paper, which relies on the talents of many people to transform the raw material into the finished article.

FROM CONCEPT TO FRUITION
Often the time that elapses between an idea being thought of and its practical application is very long indeed. But once the first steps have been taken, things can happen very quickly, as occurred in the development of civil aviation. In December 1903 the Wright Brothers showed that powered flight was attainable, and the first passenger-carrying airline began operation in January 1914.

Below are some of the things with which we are familiar today and the length of time it took to translate the concepts into tangible realities, a period which is diminished by modern technology:
– photography: more than 100 years
– the telephone: 56 years
– television: 14 years
– nuclear weapons: 6 years
– the transistor: 5 years.

Agronomists make sure that the plants are grown in the best conditions for good development and are cut at the right time.

The raw materials are taken by lorry to the factory where they will be changed into the end product.

In the factory office, executives ensure that the materials are distributed and the workload allocated.

ERGONOMICS

A rather formal definition of this comparatively new science is 'the engineering aspects of the study of the relation between human workers and their working environment.'

Put more simply, it is the study of the ways that men and women use tools and machines, and the design of new ones aimed at easier operation, reducing tiredness and making the workers more productive.

But it is not just in factories and offices that ergonomics is important. It is also used in the design of household items and accounts for the position of seats in motor vehicles, the angle of the back and head rests and the position of the various pedals and instruments.

Ergonomically designed items encourage men and women to use their bodies in the most efficient way when they are working, another example of the many ways that science can work for our benefit.

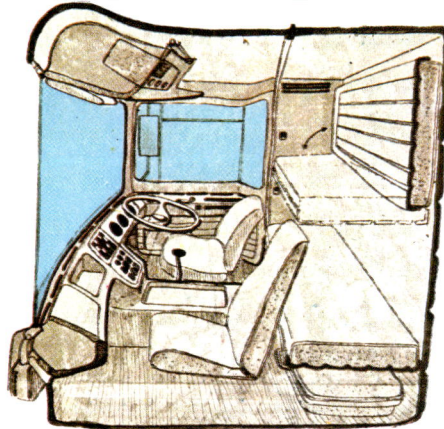

Below is a design by an Italian ergonomist for the cabin of an articulated truck. It will ensure that the driver works at optimum efficiency, and that he and his co-driver will be comfortable when at rest. The finished cabin is sketched above.

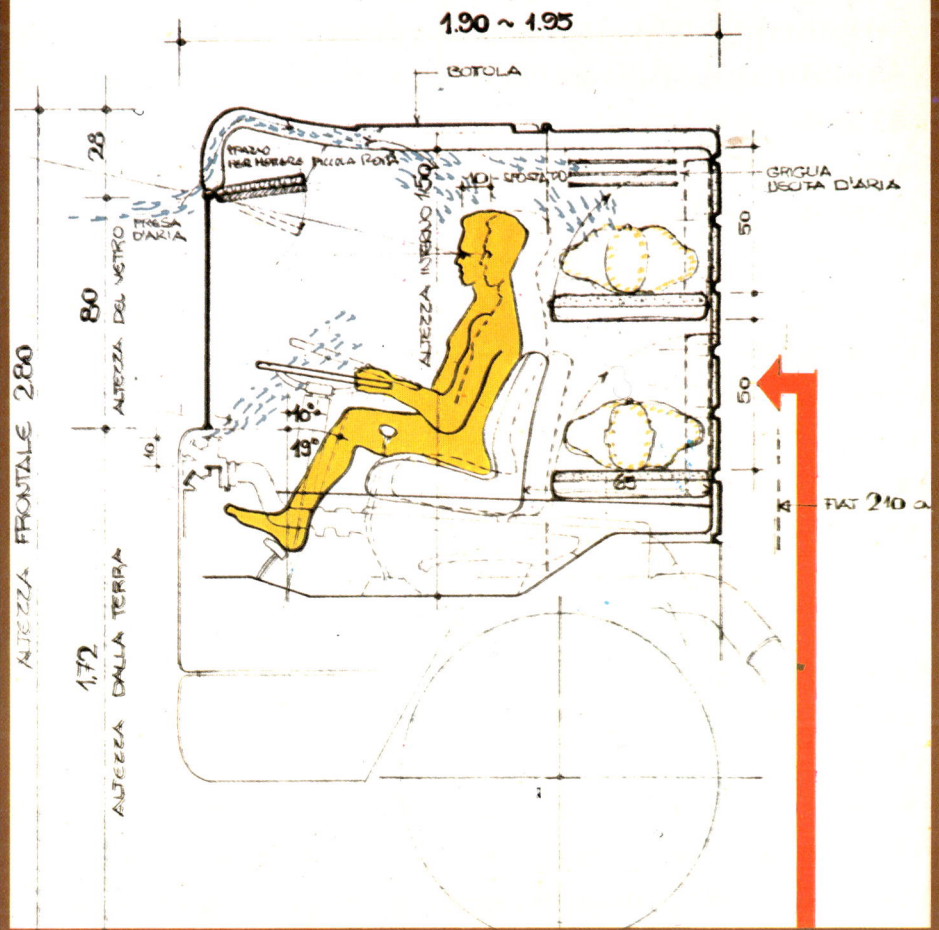

Index